MADE
IN
SPAIN

MADE IN SPAIN

A Shopper's Guide to Artisans and Their Crafts by Region

Suzanne Wales

PA PRESS

PRINCETON ARCHITECTURAL PRESS · NEW YORK

Published by
Princeton Architectural Press
A division of Chronicle Books LLC
70 West 36th Street
New York, New York 10018
papress.com

ISBN 978-1-7972-2251-6

Editor: Jennifer Thompson
Designer: Natalie Snodgrass

Library of Congress Cataloging-in-
Publication Data

Names: Wales, Suzanne, author.
Title: Made in Spain : a shopper's guide to artisans
    and their crafts by region / Suzanne Wales.
Description: First edition. | New York : Princeton
    Architectural Press, [2023] | Summary:
    "A distinctive, sumptuous, and informative guide
    to the craftspeople and artisans of Spain, with a
    focus on ceramics, paper, jewelry, leather goods,
    clothing, textiles, and shoes"
    —Provided by publisher.
Identifiers: LCCN 2022032635 (print) | LCCN
    2022032636 (ebook) | ISBN 9781797222516
    (hardcover) | ISBN 9781797224152 (ebook)
Subjects: LCSH: Artisans—Spain—Directories.
    | Shopping—Spain—Directories. |
    Handicraft industries—Spain—Directories. |
    Manufactures—Spain—Directories.
Classification: LCC TX337.S69 W35 2023
    (print) | LCC TX337.S69 (ebook) | DDC 609.2/2—
    dc23/eng/20220817
LC record available at https://lccn.loc.
    gov/2022032635
LC ebook record available at https://lccn.loc.
    gov/2022032636

CONTENTS

———

INTRODUCTION

For most people, if you ask where they are from, they will likely say the name of their country. In Spain, the common answer is first the person's town or village, followed by their region— Spaniards believe this should tell you everything you need to know.

Regional differences and personalities are at the very core of the country's history, culture, and even language. While General Franco, the dictator who ruled the country for much of the twentieth century, attempted to eradicate regional character, the return of democracy in the early 1970s brought it back with aplomb. A devolution of regional power pushed forward a revival of the social and cultural patchwork that makes Spain such a vibrant and richly nuanced destination.

This book aims to give insight into different regions of Spain celebrating its crafts and the artisans who make them. While it's true that tourism has made handmade objects widely available in shops and markets all over Spain, the stories behind each can generally be traced back to a certain village, a precise local need, a vernacular material, or a historical event that brought new skills to Iberia.

This is particularly true of Andalusia, the flamenco-infused region of southern Spain. In the tenth century, the North African colonizers brought an untold number of artisans to Al-Andalus to practice their arts in the official workshops of the caliphate. Their distinct visual language—*zellij* tile compositions, colorful, thick weave rugs, and Islamic symbolism—is still very much in favor in Andalusian craft today. The traders of the Silk Road imported the art of brocade and fan-making from Asia to Valencia, while the town of Talavera owes a proliferation of *azulejos* (hand-painted tile) workshops to its close proximity to the Royal Seat of San Lorenzo El Escorial and the Spanish kings' love of art and opulence. Bordering France, the northern region of Catalonia was the first to benefit from the industrial revolution, resulting in a sophisticated fusion of craft, design, and a more efficient approach to production. Catalan artisans of the fin de siècle worked side by side with the architects of the period, helping them forge a distinctive and labored style known as *modernisme.* The movement's intensely expressive chromatic tiles, metalwork, lead lighting, and curvaceous surfaces are endlessly reinterpreted by contemporary designers and artisans. One cannot help but notice this when walking the streets of Barcelona admiring its uniquely coherent visual style that effortlessly blends old and new.

Reinventing heritage styles is very much at the forefront of many of the second-generation artisans portrayed in this book—interested adolescents who used to hang around their parents' workshops have grown into adults who have taken over the family business. The Catalan ceramicist

Xavier Mañosa (p. 19) turned his family's small factory upside down by branching out from knickknacks into avant-garde art pottery. Elena Ferro (p. 145) tweaks traditional wooden clogs for urban contexts. While some choose to take over to save a skill from extinction, others do so for the slower, more retrospective lifestyle an artisan life provides.

Despite the abundant creativity in this book, nearly all the creators described their work simply as an *oficio*, or "trade." A lack of pretense speaks volumes in every facet of Spanish society. This endearing trait is evident in its arts and crafts, too, expressed in a cornucopia of backstories, skills, and styles that range from the humble to the sublime.

Chapter One

BARCELONA & CATALONIA

BARCELONA & CATALONIA

From the fourteenth to the sixteenth centuries, craftspeople in Barcelona and across Catalonia had a prominent place in society, the legacy of which is the city's magnificent Barri Gòtic, or Gothic Quarter. To get an idea of the extent of their old community, head to El Born, a picturesque enclave of the once walled city, where street names like Vidriera (glasswork), Argentería (metalwork), and Espartería (flax and straw) reveal the trades that once thrived here.

The next golden age of craft, and the one that Barcelona is renowned for, came at the end of the nineteenth century with *modernisme*, a Catalan variation of art nouveau. Antoni Gaudí and other architects of the period made it their mission to revive local arts and crafts, resulting in highly symbolic, labored, and thoroughly captivating landmarks such as the Casa Batlló and La Sagrada Familia.

Today, craft and design are intertwined in Barcelona. The cultural boom that was triggered by the death of the dictator Francisco Franco in 1975 resulted in another creative renaissance, and this time its language was contemporary design. Since then, Barcelona's standing as a "design city," visible in shops and architecture, signage, and even street layout, has not wavered.

Like modernisme, crafts in Catalonia today are characterized by a daring modern spin on traditional skills, coupled with plenty of imagination and a sophisticated sense of magic.

Start your deep dive into Catalan craft where it all began—in the shadowy streets of the Barri Gòtic. The Centre d'Artesania Catalunya is a government-run gallery and shop that supports local artisans. The curators have a keen eye for emerging talent, and you'll find a haven of modern design and craft that ranges from artistic glassware to daring jewelry and handmade headgear (C/ Banys Nous, 11, 08002). For craft that transcends into contemporary art and design, Il·lacions gallery is located in a palatial apartment and represents the most avant-garde of Catalan makers (p. 34). If you prefer to wander, mosey around the streets surrounding the city's cathedral for locally made ceramics, glassware, and other objects refreshingly lacking in any religious significance.

APPARATU

Passeig de la Riera, 222, Rubí, 08191
apparatu.com · tel. + 34 936 750 105

Ceramics

It's not unusual for a second generation to commandeer a family crafts business. But few change the identity and direction of the company as radically as Xavier Mañosa has.

This award-winning ceramicist is the creative director of Apparatu, a ceramics workshop on an industrial estate in Rubí, a town north of Barcelona. His parents established the company in the 1980s, producing and selling decorative terracotta pieces for neighborhood gift shops. All was well and good until the economic downturn of 2010, when many small retail businesses, gift shops included, were forced to close.

At this point, Mañosa was living in Berlin, learning German and working odd jobs far away from the craft culture he had grown up in. His mother called him with a cry for help. "My mother told me that if I wanted the business to continue then I needed to come back," says Mañosa from the mezzanine office of his atelier. "The market was changing. The question was, how do we transform?"

The answer came from Mañosa's study of industrial design, a bold approach that combined different materials into a contemporary design language, and a new company name.

Some of Apparatu's first pieces to garner admiration were white ceramic bowls with an ultra-shiny glazed interior surface in russet, red, and yellow, brightening up tables and kitchens just when we all needed it. Then came Pleat Box, a collection of pendant lamps made for Barcelonese lighting firm Marset. Made entirely of ceramics, yet with a fluid, folded fabric-like appearance, their inner surfaces are finished in either brilliant white or 24-karat gold enamel. The latter generates an extremely warm and lustrous glow, making Pleat Box a hit with smart restaurants and hotels in Barcelona. "Its shape is what has made the piece such a success," says Mañosa modestly. "And of course the material, which has a certain romance. Sewn together they create a kind of accidental formality."

Although Mañosa remains dubious of his medium's place in upper art and design echelons, this is where Apparatu has found its market. Still working with his father and a staff of eleven, he has created in-store display supports for the luxury French fashion firms Isabel Marant and Hermès and sells large-scale sculptures and stoneware podium tables through the fashionable online design and art marketplace 1st Dibs.

"For us, it's not so much the prestige of the brand," he explains, "but how we fit in with the project. We ask ourselves, what sense does it make to work with this person? Can we live with it later? When you are creating for clients, there are so many processes involved, the piece must pass through so many hands to get approved. It tests your virtuosity."

COCUAN

Plaça Nova, 5, Ripoll, 17500

cocuan.com · tel. + 34 972 539 044

Leather accessories

It is true, when one door closes another opens. This was the case with Luis Roldán, who had studied and worked as a graphic designer for twenty years, continually advancing to become a specialist in Flash, the program that once enhanced websites with sophisticated animation. When Flash became obsolete with the development of the tablet and smartphone, Roldán was in danger of becoming outdated as well.

One day he decided to make himself a ukulele, having some informal training in woodworking from his father, a professional carpenter. "The act of doing that, making something with my own hands, made me so happy," he says. "I remembered the emotion I felt helping my father out in his workshop. The same sensation just came flooding back."

After the ukulele, he made a functional, foldable leather wallet that his friends much admired. They asked him to make one for them. Then another. Like with many contemporary artisans, his business started organically among friends.

Today, Roldán trades under the name of Cocuan, a moniker for the wooden figurines his father used to make for him. Now operating in the picturesque Catalan mountain village of Ripoll, Roldán's shop and *taller* (workshop) is located on its main square. He keeps normal retail hours, including the habitual two-hour Spanish lunch break, and prefers to work alone. The chatter of local talk radio is his only companion.

"Cocuan is a lifestyle choice," says Roldán, who lives with his partner and young daughter. "We live well with very little. I don't work weekends and saying 'no' is part of Cocuan's philosophy. There is a waiting list for my products. It's rarely a problem. I will never make things in an industrial way."

What does he like about working with leather? "It's like wood—it's noble, very stable, and it has a life of its own. If it cracks, it's over, so you need to look after it well. If you grease it up every few months, it will age with you." Roldán exclusively works with a robust, full-grain leather sourced locally. He punches the holes by hand and stitches using waxed linen thread.

Roldán offers a selective collection in the Cocuan line: coin purses, pencil cases, notebook covers, belts, tool kits, and key chains. "It's for men," he adds unashamedly. He found women's bags too time-consuming, and he doesn't make phone cases anymore. "They become obsolete too quickly," as he knows all too well. "And my work is designed to last forever."

ESTUDI RIBAUDÍ

C/ del Rec, 15, Igualada, 08700
ribaudi.com · tel. + 34 938 053 458

———

Leather furniture and decor

Although surrounded by vineyards that produce grapes for Catalonia's famous cava sparkling wine, the town of Igualada prospered with another product—leather.

Once home to a thriving industry supplying horse tack to European royalty, only a few factories remain today. The historic warehouses and workshops of Rec, the neighborhood that accommodated the local leather industry, are mostly abandoned, coming alive once a year for a popular festival that celebrates its past and lets visitors scoop up work from local fashion designers at discount prices.

Jordi Ribaudí, an Igualada native, is a cofounder of the Rec festival. He is also an industrial designer for local and international firms. But his passion project is Toru—a collection of extraordinary pieces of furniture created with leather hides.

He works in an old tanning factory dating from 1850 in the Rec district. It includes a carpentry workshop for crafting frames, a sewing room with a special machine for stitching leather, and a light- and plant-filled office where he envisions his pieces. Unusually for a visual creator, Ribaudí will first conceptualize a new work with a short written text ("chasing the idea," he calls it) before moving on to a small model in paper and cardboard, and then the prototypes—a process that can take as long as two years.

Ribaudí works with thick cow and buffalo hides. He gets them tanned using vegetable extracts, which preserves their natural color and raw appearance. Ribaudí then "folds" them into shapes for chairs, stools, and other objects, which are assembled with stitching and a minimal number of wooden or metal joints and feet. The result is organic, fluid, but underscored by a proposition to consider leather's animal origin and our relationship with it. "I love the creases and imperfections of natural leather," he says. "And it's ageless. People don't know if my pieces were made five or fifty years ago."

Ribaudí makes to order, and each design has a cultural reference or eclectic symbolism. The Babu chair for example was inspired by Ribaudí's many trips to Morocco and memories of sitting on uncomfortable backless floor stools. It is constructed of a leather sheet that folds over itself to an elegant, elongated shape reminiscent of the ubiquitous *babushka* footwear of Muslim Africa. The Mimesis collection, with its ragged-edged forms, is a critique of our tendency to eat less meat. Radical? Yes. But that's the idea. "When you have your own brand, you can afford to do what you want," says Ribaudí. "I am not in competition with anyone."

MARC MONZÓ

C/ Riera de Sant Miquel, 26, Barcelona, 08006

marcmonzo.net · Representation: Hannah Gallery · hannahgallerybarcelona.net

+34 933 687 235

———————

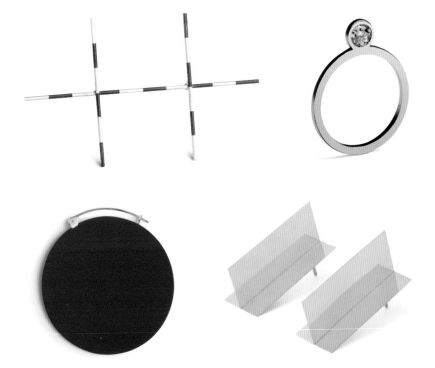

In the closed world of art jewelry, Marc Monzó is a renowned figure. Prestigious galleries all over the world represent his work, which can also be found in collections at the National Gallery of Australia and the Françoise van den Bosch Foundation in the Netherlands.

Monzó's wearable art is architectural and exquisitely executed. It is both bold and understated, with clean geometry and vivid pops of color. Sometimes the pieces resemble an *objet trouvé*, a trinket picked up from the street whose original purpose remains a delicious mystery. Many are brooches or pins, garnering Monzó a cross-genre fan base. Metal planes, S-shaped loops, and thin rods form earrings, rings, and bracelets made of gold and silver finished with enamel.

His own workshop is situated in an old industrial building in Barcelona's Poblenou district, a neighborhood where abandoned warehouses and factories now accommodate small creative start-ups. Like his work, the space is rigorously orderly, echoing Monzó's own neatly pressed appearance. A pair of hipster shoes is the only giveaway that this forty-seven-year-old is a leading figure in Barcelona's colorful art scene.

The son of an engraver, Monzó admits that he was fascinated with miniatures from a young age, spending much of his childhood making airplane models in balsa wood. His interest in jewelry awoke after seeing an exhibition by the Dutch jewelry artist Ruudt Peters. "I realized then you could express yourself in jewelry just like any other medium," he explains. "I had found my language."

Monzó then enrolled at the Escola Massana, an art school that bore many names during Barcelona's creative resurgence in the 1980 and '90s. "The philosophy of the school was a legacy of the *modernista* period," says Monzó, referring to the late-1800s artistic movement associated with Antoni Gaudí. "We were encouraged to be auteurs. To think beyond the value of materials."

Monzó uses the lost-wax casting technique, a favorite among jewelers for its level of precision. "I create the mold myself," he clarifies. "And then I get lost in the tiny details, I love them." A one-man show, Monzó creates, takes orders, and ships his work himself. I ask where he finds the time to imagine new pieces. "My inspiration comes from science, music, art," he replies. "And life itself."

MIETIS

C/ Ciutat de Granada, 62, Barcelona, 08005
mietistudio.com · tel. + 34 933 569 099

––––––––––

Leather bags and jackets

More than in any other Spanish city, craftsmanship in Barcelona comes with a strong design ethos. The role between "designer" and "artisan" is blurred, with the former channeling their voice through the latter. That said, the designer must have a strong knowledge of the medium they are working in.

Maria Fontanellas grew up surrounded by the smell and texture of luxury leather pelts. Her father owns a leather factory whose clients include Gucci and Louis Vuitton. During the school summer holidays, Fontanellas's happy place was the sample room of the factory, where new colors and textures were developed.

After studying fashion design in Milan, Fontanellas founded her leather goods brand Mietis, which was the nickname her father gave her as a child. Her designs, too, have a childlike quality, with their eye-popping, bright colors, high-contrast stitching and lining, and retro curvilinear forms. If a bag were to be in a Wes Anderson movie, Mietis would fit the role perfectly.

"I love the 1960s for its vivid colors applied to strong, clean forms," says Fontanellas from Espai Mietis, the studio and showroom she opened to develop and sell her products. Situated in Poblenou, an emerging design district, its exquisite decor bears a strong resemblance to her other acknowledged influences: the Memphis Group, who created postmodern furniture in primary block colors, and the French artist Matisse.

Fontanellas develops the prototypes for her collection in the *espai* (space) before taking them to a small workshop in Ubrique, a village in the south of Spain renowned for its leather craftsmanship. Each bag takes three days to make, and she spends several months there overseeing production. Her father developed a special finish for her products, which makes their surfaces scratch resistant; the linings are made of the same kid-soft leather as the exterior. "For start-up brands like mine, being able to produce with master craftspeople is fundamental," says Fontanellas.

The rest of her time is spent doing what any other young entrepreneur does to grow a budding fashion business, when she's not personalizing orders with bespoke color stitching and monogramming. Mietis bags retail between three hundred and five hundred euros and can only be purchased via mail order or personally at the espai. As Fontanellas explains, "For me, luxury is about craftsmanship, along with design, personalization, and the retail experience."

MERITXELL DURAN

La Rambla, 130, Barcelona, 08002.
Representation: Il·lacions Design Gallery · illacions.com · tel. + 34 649 040 672

Pottery objects

"We don't know if they came from a prehistoric past or galactic future. But wherever they go, they bring joy." This is how Catalan creator Meritxell Duran describes the pottery she handcrafts from a workshop in the middle of Montseny, a misty and mountainous natural parkland to the north of Barcelona.

In 2019, tired of city life in Barcelona, Duran moved into her ancestral family home, a handsome villa in a small Montseny village. After working as an illustrator and art teacher for most of her career, she describes her decision as an epiphany. Upon arrival, she rented a small industrial workshop with running water, a bit of natural light, and not much else. Nonetheless, it became the birthplace of her current artistic endeavor—pottery bowls, dishes, and assorted containers for sugar, soups, casseroles, and olive oil, each with a defined personality, worn-sandpaper texture, and endearing off-kilter charm.

"The idea behind the objects is a bit *casa de payes*," explains Duran, referring to the cave-like stone farmsteads that are not only a physical feature of the Catalan countryside, but also a representation of its ancient culture. "I want them to gather dust. In fact, because of their porous surface, they will never be clean." Nor will they be "perfect," a condition Duran describes as "the greatest human error." She adds, "When we look at perfect objects, we only just skim the surface. We don't go deep."

With the same visual style Duran developed as an illustrator, she sketches ideas for her objects in simple kraft paper notebooks that she always carries with her. But when she arrives at her studio, Duran never has a clear idea of what she is going to do, preferring to let each piece pop up almost magically.

Working on about five pieces at a time, she first molds the base, then the "lid." Their quirky faces, with their bulging eyes and pursed lips, come last, before the pieces are sent off for firing and then glazing, which she applies to their interior surface only, making them suitable for serving and storing foodstuffs.

Duran uses grog (also known as firesand or chamotte) to give form to her pieces but has recently been experimenting with other materials, such as porcelain, which she may use to make contrasting lids for her collections. However, it's unlikely that any developments will veer too far off from her established language, or indeed, that their lids align with their base in a snap. "I like the fact it takes a second or two to get the lids into place," she says. "It makes us focus on the act. We lose so much by multitasking."

NORMAN VILALTA

C/ d'Enric Granados, 5, Barcelona, 08007
normanvilalta.com · tel. + 34 933 234 014

Bespoke men's shoes

A few minutes' walk from the Passeig de Gràcia, the bustling avenue of Gaudí attractions and international brand boutiques, is the Carrer d'Enric Granados—a quiet, leafy, and much less touristy street named after a Catalan classical pianist. Down at its southern end where the pavement widens before morphing into the gardens of the old university, you will find a few outdoor cafes, a skate shop, and the storefront of Norman Vilalta, maker of luxurious men's shoes.

Even if you are not in the market for a pair of handmade Chelsea boots, oxfords, or loafers, you can't help peering in the front window. At the back of the store, past the podiums displaying footwear finished with subtle patinas, swirls of perforated details, and almond-shaped toes, Vilalta sits on a low stool at a wooden bench. Bottles of tints, jars of brushes, dozens of carved shoe lasts, and a greater number of aged traditional cobbler tools surround him.

Vilalta didn't start out as a shoemaker and says that he is really not interested in shoes—he only possesses two or three pairs himself. It's the possibilities of the craft that fascinate him, and the creation of a thing of beauty. "Absolutely everything is in a pair of shoes," he declares.

Born in Buenos Aires, Argentina, Vilalta knew from a young age that he was good with his hands. Despite this, he studied law and worked in the corporate world for more than two decades, albeit in a "very humanist practice," he assures us. "I learned about metaphysics, theology, and philosophy. I learned to question the rules."

In 2004, he transferred to Florence, Italy, to learn the craft of shoemaking with a number of maestros, including the renowned shoemaker Stefano Bemer. Vilalta is elusive when asked why he then moved to Barcelona but cites the ancient heritage of the craft in the city, and the graves in the city's cathedral of the heads of the medieval shoemaker's guild. Nonetheless, with a donation of old cobbler's tools from an orthopedic shoemaker, a place to work, and the observation that Spanish men's shoes available at the time were really quite ugly, he set up a bespoke shoe business.

Vilalta remembers his first customer, "a dandy from Valencia who wanted a pair of shoes to wear to a wedding." He laughs off, but doesn't deny, a rumor that he makes shoes for the king of Spain.

There is a waiting list of a year for a pair of his bespoke shoes, which requires a personal fitting, a made-to-order last, and a trial shoe before delivery of the finished product, a process that comes at a cost of around 3,500 euros.

Realizing that it was a limited market, in 2014 Vilalta launched a ready-to-wear line with a starting price of one thousand euros. Although made in a small workshop in La Rioja, the ready-to-wear boots and shoes are hand-finished in his Barcelona atelier, using the same painstaking methodology as the bespoke models, and to the same faultless standards. Deep color gradients, subtle textural variations, and architectural accents on classical forms define his creations. "Every pair of shoes has to have a strong idea behind it," he asserts. "The only tradition I believe in is to innovate."

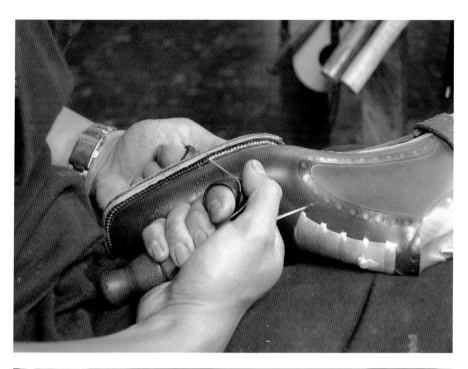

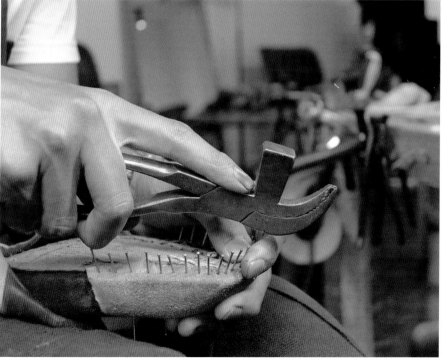

OCTAEVO

C/ Llull, 48–52, 5–3, Barcelona, 08005

octaevo.com

———

Stationery and objects

One summer Marcel Baer, art director, graphic designer, and founder of the Barcelona-based company Octaevo, participated in a ceramics workshop in the village of La Bisbal d'Empordá, the epicenter of the pottery industry in Catalonia. He attempted to make a vase using a pottery wheel but gave up. He then tried rolling the clay into sheets, without success. He then started playing with the shape of the vase he desired with pieces of stiff paper. He cut out a classic urn shape in two parts and stitched both sides together. This experiment became the signature piece of his company— a flat vase made of water-resistant paper and printed with Baer's colorful designs. Users slide it over a cut-off plastic water bottle to add volume and make it suitable for displaying fresh flowers.

Mediterranean travel and culture—two things Baer feels a strong connection to—is the narrative running through Octaevo. With names like "Riviera" and "Stromboli," and vibrant palettes of burnt orange and Yves Klein blue contrasted with gold brushstrokes, Octaevo's design objects hint at a time of Mediterranean discovery. With a forthright postmodern twist, their patterns reference Capri sunsets and Roman tiles, classic Greek statuary, and marble arches and floors.

Baer was born to a Swiss father and a Spanish mother, and Mediterranean travel was always part of his family's life. "My father was an engineer who worked at sea and my grandfather was a pilot," he explains. "I have some amazing old photographs of them traveling to exotic places." Similarly, his love of paper comes from a childhood holiday memory, namely passing by a stationery store in a Valencian village on his way to buy ice cream.

Each piece in the Octaevo collection tells a story. "The collections work together," explains Baer. "Creating a universe, or kind of 'Atlas of the Med.'" He describes product development as a slow, organic process. New "families" are drip-fed onto his website, and recently he has branched into other materials such as gelato-colored candles made in a local workshop. Paper objects, however, such as linen-covered notebooks, marble-lined envelopes, and Octaevo's bestselling vase, will remain predominant. "I have always been especially interested in the possibilities of print," he assures us.

PARDOhats

C/ Santa Eulàlia, 29, Barcelona, 08012
pardohats.com · tel. + 34 722 832 242

———————

Millinery

While each of Barcelona's neighborhoods has a unique character, Gràcia is one of its most charming. Once a separate village, Gràcia's fiery history is one of workers collectives and unionism, small-scale workshops and crafts. Today many of the storefronts are occupied by a new generation of creatives. People like the hatmaker Sol Pardo.

Despite the blistering summer sun, Spaniards are not particularly fond of covering their heads. Nonetheless, Pardo's hats are regularly featured in Spain's glossy press and fashion events. With double brims, earth-colored patterns, and shell or raffia trim, they possess a boho feel, making them perfect for the Instagram-able, hippie-chic vibe of Spain's island culture.

Although she is a milliner of the moment, Pardo never intended to be one. She grew up in a creative family in Buenos Aires. Her grandfather was an artist of considerable repute, and anything other than a creative career was not considered. "I was diagnosed with dyslexia," she reveals. "So my artistic skills were really nurtured. I felt I didn't have a choice."

Pardo studied scenic arts, which led to her love of costume and then fashion design. It was happenstance, however, that led her to the world of hats. During a student fashion parade, the magazine *Harper's Bazaar* picked up on one of her headpieces, in her words "an ugly sequined baseball cap." Suddenly she was a hatmaker.

After learning the craft with Argentina's society milliner Laura Noetinger, she traveled to Europe, where she found her market and realized that fashion had an anthropological aspect. "In Argentina, women think that fashion is for bimbos," she opines. "It's not. It can be an intellectual pursuit."

From her mezzanine atelier, Pardo, who believes that stock is waste, makes all her hats to order. Starting with the molds, which Pardo carves herself in cork, she works exclusively with natural materials such as straw, wool, leather, and organic pigments. Nothing in her creations is synthetic, even the glue. "I love the fact that I can make a high-fashion product with cheap, organic materials," she says. "My generation is changing the definition of luxury."

TEIXIDORS

C/ Mare de Déu dels Àngels, 131, Terrassa, 08221

teixidors.com · tel. + 34 937 831 199

———————

Handwoven textiles

Teixidors makes luxurious home textiles and shawls on replicas of nineteenth-century looms. The company was started as a social experiment, and its weavers are intellectually disabled.

The Catalan town of Terrassa is situated twelve miles inland from Barcelona. When the train line from Barcelona to Terrassa was completed in 1856, a prosperous industrial era was born whose principal activity was textiles. This lasted until the outbreak of Spain's civil war. Today there are only a few companies left.

Teixidors is situated in a majestic old textile factory, where the rhythmic click-clack of more than twenty traditional wooden weaving looms echoes around the building's soaring vaulted ceiling. If it weren't for the modern dress of the weavers and finishing and sorting staff, it could easily be a scene from the heyday of Terrassa's industrial revolution.

Teixidors's own history is much more recent. The company was founded in 1983 by Juan Ribás, a textile engineer, and Marta Ribás, a social worker who, inspired by a similar project she had seen in Sweden, had a vision to give work and dignity to intellectually disabled adults. The weaving process, with its high degree of repetition and attention to detail, was considered a good fit. However, the level of creativity and craftsmanship reached by Teixidors goes way beyond the definition of "remedial."

"It's not really fair to define our weavers as 'disabled,'" explains Joanna Thörnblad, director of Teixidors. "They are experts in what they do. It's very difficult to find the level of quality and craftsmanship anywhere."

There is a hushed, monastic ambience as she leads me through the weaving room, where sixteen weavers concentrate on warp and weft configurations that produce Teixidors products. It takes about an hour

to weave a meter of fabric. The contrasting color edges are intricate and time-consuming but have become a brand signature.

The weavers principally work in cashmere, merino, and, more recently yak yarn. The merino wool comes from a small flock in Provence, France, while the yak and cashmere are sourced from a cooperative in Mongolia as part of the company's commitment to sustainability. The yarns are spun into throws, blankets, and shawls, either for contract commissions for interior design projects, or for boutiques in Spain, Europe, and the US.

"We aim for the luxury market. We made a decision early on to invest in materials and design," continues Thörnblad. Special collections for renowned designers such as John Pawson and Faye Toogood have recently pushed the creative and technical capacity of the company in terms of patterns, textures, and color gradient. "This level of client demands perfection and so do we," Thörnblad declares. "What we are doing here is unique. We can definitely compete with the best."

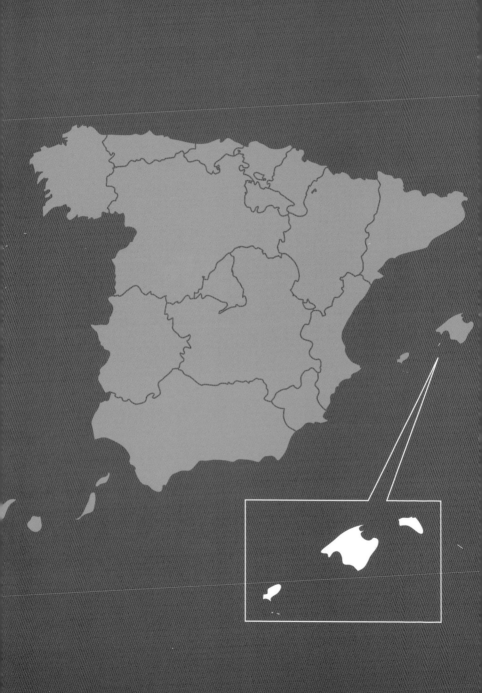

Chapter Two

BALEARIC ISLANDS

BALEARIC ISLANDS

O ff the coast of northeastern Spain, Mallorca, Menorca, Ibiza, and Formentera are collectively known as the Balearic Islands. Their strategic location at the crossroads of the Mediterranean have made them the target of numerous colonizers, from the Greeks and Romans to the Turks and the British, whose Royal Navy briefly took possession of Menorca in 1713. Many would argue that they haven't left, as the islands, particularly Ibiza and Mallorca, are hugely popular destinations for northern hemisphere sun seekers who pack the coastal resorts over the summer months.

It's the workaday inland regions, however, where the real treasures of the islands are to be found. This is particularly true of Mallorca, the largest of the archipelago. Its varied landscape, from mountains to fertile plains bursting with cereal, fruit, and olive crops, and culturally rich villages and towns, paints a much more industrious and cosmopolitan picture than the rest of the islands. Until recently, Mallorca was the epicenter of Spain's important footwear industry. The *alpargata*, a flat-soled, tie-up espadrille, is a sartorial symbol of Mallorca and seen everywhere in a myriad of colorful and textural variations. For fine leather footwear,

the pretty township of Inca still has a number of outlet
and factory shops from top Spanish brands. During tourist
season, all the islands host "hippie markets" near the beaches
and ports. While they are not quite the countercultural
gatherings they were in the 1970s, you can still find jewelry,
textiles, and other knickknacks crafted by local makers.

Palma de Mallorca, the island's capital, is best known for
high-end craft and design, particularly in the boutiques of
the central district and around the Passeig del Born. Be on
the lookout for artful goblets, water jugs, and *aceiteras* (oil
and vinegar dispensers) by Gordiola, a company that has
been blowing glass on the island since 1719.

Marlene Albaladejo is part of the family who founded
the luxury brand Carmina Shoemaker (p. 75). She owns
La Pecera, an expertly curated shop in central Palma
(C/ de la Victòria, 4, 07001), which retails locally handmade
objects and furniture. "I think every Spanish region has its
own creative language. But here it's characterized by a lot
of natural materials, light, color, and *mar y muntaña* (sea
and mountain) contrast," she says, referring to the unique
variation of landscape in Mallorca. "Being an island, we are
not so influenced by trends. The artistic style here is more
pure and rational. We need to nurture it!"

XAVIER MONCLÚS

C/ Rector Mort, 22B, Maó, 07701, Menorca
klimt02.net/jewellers/xavier-monclus · tel. + 34 695 888 300

Artistic jewelry

Xavier Monclús is a generous man who makes brooches, pendants, and objects with a lot of heart. Originally from Barcelona, where he studied at the famed Escola Massana art school, Monclús settled on the tiny and wildly picturesque island of Menorca in 2013. "Not many people know this," notes Monclús, "but Menorca was once the center of costume-making in Spain."

While Monclús's artistic language shares some of the originality and modernity of costume jewelry, it has more to do with his obsession as a collector of miniature toys, which includes Matchbox and Dinky diecast cars, Laurel and Hardy figures, and Pipo—the tiny Spanish "smoking doll" from the 1950s. Monclús's jewelry is also objects in miniature. Childlike animals and the whitewashed, vernacular architecture of Menorca are recurring themes.

He was originally attracted to jewelry-making for its high level of craftsmanship and materiality. "I love the way you can manipulate the materials with so many methods," he explains. "From smelting to cutting, filing and soldering. Then I add unusual elements—wood, found objects, and collage. I think this part comes from my love of toys."

Monclús first cuts the pattern in silver before constructing the three-dimensional piece, which is enclosed around a central void. Then with minuscule drills and files he engraves the textures and details—the rough surfaces of bricks, the grain of a rustic wooden door, or the patterns of palm fronds. Once this step is completed, he paints the figures with epoxy resin. "The most difficult is the white 'walls,'" he remarks. "Every little error is exposed."

Monclús's endearing creations can be found in museum collections and are sold in specialist jewelry galleries and shops. Each one can take two to three weeks to complete, though Monclús often works on two at a time so as "not to get bored." And how does he feel when they are finally finished? "It's like giving birth," he says with a big belly laugh.

STUDIO JAIA

Costa de Can Muntaner, 5, Local 2, La Palma de Mallorca, 07003
studiojaia.com · tel. + 34 642 585 415

————

Furniture

The stunning island of Mallorca, famed for its intimate beaches, glittering marinas, and mountainous interior, supports a cozy and diverse artistic community. Craft and design shops dot the old town of Palma de Mallorca, the island's capital, and in every rustic hilltop village you can encounter the wares of a local shoemaker or basket maker. Alongside established crafts, a growing number of young makers are reinterpreting traditional skills in contemporary ways.

Anna Lena Kortmann trained as an architect. She moved from Berlin to Mallorca in 2013 for its scenery and lifestyle. She soon became fascinated with woven rattan furniture, a ubiquitous style of decor found all over Spain and especially on the islands. "Coming from an architectural background, I guess I was just attracted to the patterns and geometry," she says. Kortmann found an artisan who agreed to give her informal lessons and she started tinkering around with materials, patterns, and shapes. Studio Jaia, whose name is affectionately argot for "grandmother," was born.

Kortmann gives a contemporary twist to the craft with lightweight, modern, angular forms and soft pastel colors by replacing rattan with fine cotton cord. She makes each piece from concept up. First, she cuts and constructs the frame before weaving the seat or back directly onto it— the part of the process she enjoys the most. "I have gotten really hooked on weaving and breaking the lines down one by one to make a form." Kortmann creates the patterns herself. "I constantly sketch and develop, often just tweaking little details in traditional patterns I have seen." It takes a full day of weaving to create the smallest piece in Studio Jaia's

collection—the puput stool. Her natural patience and perfectionism, she confesses, is a virtue.

All Studio Jaia pieces are made to order and take about six weeks to deliver. Although Kortmann is considering outsourcing the frame-making to a carpenter, her midrange goal is to continue producing in a slow, local, and sustainable way. "Knowing that each piece turns out exactly how I want it is the most satisfying part of what I do."

ADRIANA MEUNIÉ

C/ Mar, 26, Felantrix, 07200, Mallorca

adrianameunie.wordpress.com · tel. + 34 722 203 416 · By appointment only

---

Textile art

From the outside, Adriana Meunié appears to live the perfect island life. This bubbly thirty-two-year-old is a Mallorca native. She lives in an artsy, boho farmhouse in the countryside with her partner, the noted ceramicist Jaume Roig, and twenty sheep. Her flock provides some of the raw material for her artwork, which she creates inside an old carriage house in the medieval village of Felanitx. When I comment that all this sounds like heaven, she laughs, adding, "Most people don't know what it's really like to live in the countryside."

Meunié studied fashion design in Barcelona but soon became disillusioned with the industry. She describes the development of her artistic language, which she expresses in "textile pictures," as extremely slow and involving a lot of experimentation.

I ask her what exactly she means by a "textile picture." She admits, "I also have trouble defining that. But to me they are pictures, they are not woven. I start with a base of canvas and I work from there, adding form and volume with natural fibers."

Meunié's "pictures" are raw and primordial. The fibers she uses—wool, rope, reeds, and esparto grass—are attached to the canvas one strand at a time, a painfully slow and meticulous process that can be appreciated when you look at the back of the canvas and see a dense matrix of knots. On the other side, the fibers cascade and dance. Pagan folk rituals and ancient crop circles come to mind.

It's an aesthetic that is currently à la mode. Meunié is in demand for site-specific commissions from architects and lifestyle brands, including the Spanish luxury fashion brand Loewe and the five-star resort designer Toni Esteva. "I think I started at a good time, because now there is a growing understanding of craft within the art world," she reflects. "But I also think there is a lot of confusion on what is art, what craft is, and what is design. I consider myself an artist who is learning. An artist isn't born. You learn to be one, just like every other job, no?"

HUGUET

C/ Cami Vell de Ciutat, 33, Campos, 07630, Mallorca

huguetmallorca.com · tel. + 34 971 650 609

––––––––

Handmade tiles

Enduringly charming and popular, *suelo hidráulico*, or patterned cement floor tiles, are a decorative symbol of Catalonia and the Balearic Islands. It was the early nineteenth-century *modernista* architects who introduced them as a cheaper and more durable alternative to mosaic flooring. They made them a mainstay of their fanciful apartments and palaces, blanketing each room in different variations, combinations, and color schemes. Still today, whether newly minted or restored, suelo hidráulico tiles are still very much in fashion in interior design circles for their infinite design possibilities and sheer loveliness.

Huguet puts a contemporary spin on traditional suelo hidráulico. Founded in 1933 in Mallorca, it is one of the hundred or so manufacturers originally on the island. Most closed down during the cheap construction boom of the 1960s and '70s, which saw a return to more functional and bland floor coverings for the high-rise apartments that appeared when tourism took off. Huguet hung on by switching from making tiles to concrete beams, until Biel Huguet, grandson of the founder and a trained architect, took over the business in 1997.

He came with a mission to revive the art of the tile in a more modern context by offering a bespoke service to architects and designers who could create their own collections. Herzog & de Meuron, Alfredo Häberli, and Elias Torres are just some of the renowned names who have put their signature to Huguet tiles.

While the aesthetic has changed, the production method at Huguet remains the same as it did a century go. Square metal molds are filled with a layer of sand and cement, which forms the base and creates durability. On top of this is placed a handmade metal stencil, into which artisans pour

a liquid compound of finer cement, marble powder, and pigment to form a pattern. The tiles are then flattened with a hydraulic press and left to dry before being polished to a creamy luster.

Instead of the curly, romantic patterns in traditional suelo hidráulico, Huguet's tile collections feature bold, robust, and abstract motifs. But when it comes to creating a new design, as the company confirms, the possibilities are endless.

MAJORAL

Avinguda de la Mola, 89, El Pilar de la Mola, 07872, Formentera

majoral.com · tel. + 34 971 327 516

————————

Fine jewelry

With its pristine natural harbors, salt pans, and clusters of pine and juniper forests, tiny Formentera is the archetypal western Mediterranean island. Yet many visitors to the Balearic region are unaware of its existence until they arrive. Formentera has managed to retain the alternative lifestyle the Balearics were famous for before the designer hotels and boutiques moved in.

After extensive travels in India in what he calls a hippie bus, Enric Majoral, a self-taught jeweler and metal craftsman, relocated to Formentera in the late 1970s with his wife, the photographer Dolors Ballester. He cofounded what is now the island's most famous man-made attraction, the La Mola Arts and Crafts Market, an outdoor market where artisans sell wares at sunset against the stunning backdrop of La Mola peninsula. With limited resources and few tools, Majoral at first made metal belt buckles, and then brooches, earrings, and necklaces inspired by the flora and fauna of the island.

As business grew, the couple decided to open a retail shop in Barcelona, with the idea of living winters in the city and summers in their paradise island home. Drawing from a more urban context steeped in the traditions of surrealism, his pieces became geometric and avant-garde, coinciding with the postmodern artistic trends in Barcelona in the early 1980s. "When we opened the shop there wasn't really any alternative to classical jewelry," says Majoral. "It was still considered quite elitist."

Four decades later, Mayoral is widely considered an exemplary brand not only in modern jewelry but also in Spanish design and maker culture. The studio's methods have evolved into the most sophisticated processes and a recognizable DNA that is undeniably contemporary but

also timeless and poetic. Sometimes the studio's works have the appearance of bronze-age artifacts, at others a natural pearl submerged in a sea of molten silver. All are underlined by a connection to the Mediterranean and its ancient cultures, creatures, and topographies.

Now Enric Majoral is seventy-four years old, and his son Roc co-creates the fifteen to twenty new designs the studio produces each year and sells around the world. "Our aim is still to bring the art of jewelry closer to the people," continues Majoral. "To those that appreciate a different form of expression."

TEIXITS RIERA

C/ Major, 50, Lloseta, 07360, Mallorca

riera.com · tel. + 34 971 514 034

Ikat textiles

Ikat fabric originated in Indonesia then traveled to the Mediterranean and beyond via the traders on the Silk Road. On the island of Mallorca, the fabric has been popular in home decor since the early 1900s. Back then it was created in small workshops all over the island. Artisans put their own sunny stamp on the cotton textile, swapping traditional indigo-blue-and-terracotta backgrounds for cream and white, and dyeing the contrasting yarns in softer colors such as frothy green, yellow, and aqua blue. They even developed their own ikat pattern. The *roba de llengües* (cloth of tongues) is a zig-zaggy design that represents the craggy landscape of the island's Serra de Tramuntana mountain range. Ikat was popular for wall coverings, curtains, and upholstery among the island's upper classes, who bought bolts of the fabric from traveling salesmen, often just storing it away for posterity.

Gabriel Riera is the great grandson of one such ikat entrepreneur. Today he runs Teixits Riera, an artisan manufacturer of ikat cloth and home textiles, a business that was founded by his great grandfather in 1893. "I sometimes have clients come into our shop with a piece of fabric telling me, 'Look! I bought this seventy years ago! It's been stuffed away in a drawer all this time.'"

The dynamic patterns in ikat are formed by dyeing the yarn *prior* to weaving, unlike other dyeing and printing processes. Following a design blueprint, artisans tightly bind sausage-like bundles of yarn before dipping them into the dye vats. Once dried under the sun, the bindings are removed, and the threads are woven on a loom. The characteristic blurriness of ikat patterns is a result of the weavers trying to exactly match up the dyed sections of the thread—an impossible task.

Like many small-scale artisans, Riera says that finding people committed to learning the laboriously meticulous ikat processes can be a challenge. At full capacity, his workshop can produce fifty meters of fabric a day. But beyond this, he thinks his biggest challenge is establishing Mallorcan ikat as unique and culturally significant. "It's a very different kind of fabric and it has a long line of tradition behind it," he says. "I hope that when people touch it, they can appreciate its history."

CARMINA SHOEMAKER

C/ de la Unió, 4, Palma de Mallorca, 07001

carminashoemaker.com · tel. + 34 971 229 047

Handmade footwear

With its scarlet red facade, bold brass signage, and lush art deco interior, the Carmina Shoemaker flagship store in Palma de Mallorca draws as many onlookers as the city's historical attractions—which in many ways it is one.

Shoemaking has a long tradition in Mallorca. In the early 1900s, when the phylloxera plague devastated the island's vineyards, many locals turned to leather tanning and shoemaking. Business boomed along with tourism, until the 1980s when labor costs and logistical considerations forced companies to move overseas or to the mainland. Spain's important footwear industry is now centered in Alicante, in the south of the country. Out of the four hundred or so Mallorca shoe manufacturers of the past, only four remain today.

In 1866, Carmina Shoemaker was established in the town of Inca, the epicenter of the island's shoe industry, by Matias Pujadas. A decade later, he was joined by his son Mateo, who introduced the Goodyear shoe welting technique into the factory. This innovation led to greater durability and ease of resoling, making his shoes popular with farmers and workers toiling the rough Mallorcan terrain.

In the 1960s Mateo's grandson José joined the company, bringing with him Italian design training and a vision to transform the company, which he named after his wife, Carmina, into a prestige handcrafted shoe brand.

Lasting durability is still a feature of the classically elegant loafers, oxfords, Chelseas, and dress boots crafted by Carmina Shoemaker. The brand's signature leather is cordovan, a famously tough skin from a horse bred in the south of Spain and originally used for armory.

Production methods at Carmina Shoemaker's small factory have changed little over time: patterns are hand-traced, lasts hand-carved, shoes stitched one by one and then worked into subtle multitone patinas with ermine hairbrushes. The factory produces about fifty thousand pairs a year, with bespoke orders taking between forty-five to sixty days.

Carmina Shoemaker has shops in New York, Madrid, Barcelona, Paris, and Dubai, and a client list that includes international film stars and European royalty. Despite such wide-reaching appreciation, the company remains staunchly local and intent on keeping production of its renowned footwear firmly on Mallorcan soil.

Chapter Three

VALENCIA

VALENCIA

O nce a year in March, Valencia is on fire, both literally and figuratively. The billows of smoke and bursts of flame that float over the city are caused by the festival Las Fallas. Originally a tribute to Saint Joseph, it has come to express the quirks of the region—a love of the baroque, a high tolerance for loud noise, and a taste for irreverence and caricature.

The main event of Las Fallas is the public torching of grotesque papier-mâché effigies of politicians, sports stars, celebrities of the moment, or anyone deemed worthy of a good lampooning. Many of them have been sculpted by local ceramics artisans—a medium for which Valencia is renowned and has historically excelled in. Further proof of this can be found at the city's Museo Nacional de Cerámica, a gloriously excessive baroque palace that displays a feast of locally made decorative art in porcelain and pottery.

From fire to silk, UNESCO has recognized Valencia as part of the ancient Silk Road (the silk trade drove the region's golden age). During Las Fallas, local women dress up in traditional swag crafted in *espolín*, a rich silk brocade that has for centuries robed priests and aristocracy throughout

Europe. You'll see it, or references to it, everywhere in Valencia. From lovely purses and shoes in touristy shops in the *casco antiguo* (old town) to hand-painted tiles decorating building facades and fountains. Many of these were made in Manises, a Valencian village famous for ceramics production since the fourteenth century. Nowadays students come to study at its internationally renowned Escola d'Art i Superior de Ceràmica, while locals pick up exquisite chromatic tiles for their homes directly from manufacturers. The Valencian company Lladró is the most famous name in Spanish porcelain, with legions of fans all over the world. You'll see their objects, which range from charmingly kitsch to imaginative, pop art concoctions, in shops everywhere. Situated close to the city of Valencia in the town of Tavernes Blanques, the company's workshop facilities can also be visited by appointment. For more everyday artisan wares, the shops and stalls around Valencia's Mercat Central—a magnificent structure lined with luscious tile work—are worth exploration.

More than the residents of many other Spanish cities, Valencianos are sticklers for tradition. The city has hung on to, somewhat stubbornly, features of "old school" Spain. The same tenacity is evident in its artisan culture that, through a combination of reinvention and sheer tenacity, is keeping local craft alive.

VICENTE GRACIA JOYAS

C/ de la Paz, 4, Valencia, 46003

vicentegraciajoyas.com · tel. + 34 963 510 618

———

Fine jewelry

Vicente Gracia is known as the "poet jeweler." His establishment, situated in a townhouse in a posh, central shopping street, seems to have stepped out from a former, more gracious world. For that matter, so does Gracia. Habitually dressed in an immaculate suit with a dapper silk handkerchief folded into his jacket pocket, he greets clients on the upper floor in his showroom office, an exquisite room laden with antique books, fine art, and eclectic ephemera. An array of his extraordinary rings, earrings, and necklaces are displayed in glass domes and dioramas, but mostly Gracia makes to order. Clients who include Spanish nobility and wives of American tech magnates sit down at a large drawing table as Gracia paints a proposal on parchment paper using watercolor. Once a design is approved, it is crafted in the atelier at the rear of the showroom. It is then delivered in a handmade velvet box lined with local *espolín*, the fine damask that made its way to Valencia via the Silk Road that is one of Gracia's passions.

Born in Valencia, Gracia's father was a successful silversmith of hunting trophies and traditional tableware. Gracia grew up fascinated with silverware processes but knew his language was more contemporary. Escola Massana, the famed art and design school in Barcelona, helped him discover his voice. Gracia studied there at the time of *La Movida Madrileña*—the cultural awakening that ignited a newly democratic Spain during the mid-to-late 1980s. "Barcelona was really the birthplace of La Movida," says Gracia. "My teachers were Antoni Tàpies and Joan Miró. This was what I related to."

Later in his career, Gracia found that his main influence would be more spiritual and rooted in Spain's pre-Christian history. "Sufism, the mystical dimension of Islam, has been really important to me over the years," he confides. "For me, Sufi philosophy is the Silk Road, a rising desert moon, the bejeweled Andalus garden of emerald leaves and garnet roses."

To illustrate his point, Gracia pulls out a ring whose inspiration comes from a Sufi poem, "Gulistan" (The Rose Garden). Lightweight, despite its size, the ring depicts a curled burst of leaves carved in emeralds, with opal, garnet, and pink tourmaline buds woven together with tiny enamel birds at its exquisite base.

Gracia almost exclusively works with matte gold, a material he describes as "more expressive" than any alternative. Sometimes he is asked to refashion a family heirloom, such as such as a pair of diamond earrings he transformed into three rings for the owner's great-grandchildren. "What we do here is create dreams," he says. "Jewelry is the only art form where sentiment is more important than the actual object."

ANA ILLUECA CERAMICS

C/ Rodrigo de Pertegás, 42, Valencia, 46023

anaillueca.com · tel. + 34 645 202 626

Ceramics

When walking around Valencia's *casco antiguo*, you may notice that a lot of the doors guarding medieval buildings are made of bronze. All of them display an uneven green patina, the result of exposure to sea air over the centuries.

The ceramicist Ana Illueca has made that oxidized green part of her creative signature. She is a member of a handful of largely self-taught local ceramicists who are going against the swirly, baroque "Manises" style of ceramics that Valencia is famous for. "When I started doing this, Valencian ceramics hadn't been updated for decades, and artisans were disappearing," she says from her light-filled studio near the city's ragtag port. Illueca studied graphic design and was a hobbyist potter. Seven years ago she left her job as an art director of a well-regarded creative agency to study artistic ceramics made famous by Escola d'Art i Superior de Ceràmica. "I could conceptualize pieces but had no idea how to make them," she confesses. "The course was extremely taxing, but at the end of the day you understand it's a skill like any other."

Illueca exclusively uses a potter's wheel and oversees every stage of the process. She experiments with mixing pigments and glazes—both are exacting skills that even small-production potters often outsource. "I suppose I could just make plates, or buy premade glazes," she says. "But my technical knowledge is my point of difference. The more you have, the more you can develop your language."

Illueca describes her language as "Contemporary Mediterranean," or "folkloric in a modern way." Her most recent collection is titled *Barbecho*—a Latin term that refers to the agricultural process of leaving fields to fallow between crops. It was conceived during Spain's protracted COVID-19 lockdown, when the entire country was in a state of enforced idleness (i.e., fallow). Impeccably turned in high-quality gray clay with a robust cylindrical form, the pieces are hand-painted with abstract shapes in cobalt, yellow, and her signature oxidized green that resemble ancient crop markings.

"People are definitely wanting larger, more meaningful pieces," she says when asked about trends in art pottery. "I always have a shape in mind when I sit down at the wheel. That said, you never really know what will appear when you open the oven door."

ABANICOS VIBENCA VICENTE BENLLOCH CABALLER

Plaza de Lope de Vega, 5, Valencia, 46001
abanicosvibenca.com · tel. + 34 690 192 055

Hand-painted fans

Abanicos (fans) are as native to Valencia as oranges. Although they are more associated with the foot-tapping flamenco culture of southern Spain, fans arrived in the seventeenth century from the East to Valencia, which stood at the end of the Silk Road. Craftspeople will proudly tell you that the entire fan-making industry has long been based in the Valencia region, from small workshops that produce the ribs to homeworkers specialized in creating elaborate leaves with lace and embroidery.

Now most abanicos you see in tourist shops are imported. Very few of the traditional fan shops and makers remain.

Squirrelled away in the heart of Valencia's *casco antiguo*, Vicente Benlloch is one of the last traditional fan painters in Valencia. He works from a cramped workroom at the rear of his shop. Hunched over his work-table, he paints up to thirty fans a day, mostly with traditional floral motifs and a few forays into colorful abstract patterns.

"Like many artisans, I learned how to do this by looking over my father's shoulder," says Benlloch. He pulls down a black-and-white photo from the wall that shows his father studiously painting a fan with the young, angel-faced Benlloch dressed in the traditional school smock of the era, staring directly at the camera. His father learned the craft from his own father, who founded the business in 1910. Benlloch moved to his business's current location, a handsome corner storefront, in 2015.

Groups of tourists regularly stop to peer through the large windows to see Benlloch at work. He is happy for them to come inside to take a closer look and find out more about his craft. Some buy, many don't. "Of course, I would prefer if they did," he says. "But if they take home some knowledge about fan-making and spread that around, I am okay with that too."

GARIN 1820

C/ de Ramon Villarroya, 15, Montcada, 46113, Valencia
garin1820.com · tel. + 34 961 309 023

Handwoven silk

Silk came to Spain via traders along the ancient Silk Road as part of the Islamic expansion over the Mediterranean. By the fifteenth century, it was one of Valencia's principal sources of income, traded at the magnificent La Lonja de la Seda (Silk Exchange), which remains one of the city's most celebrated gothic structures. By the eighteenth century, more than five thousand looms in the city were supplying royal courts, the clergy, and European aristocracy with luxurious damasks, brocades, and a tightly woven, floral-patterned silk known as *espolín*, a fabric that carries Valencian history and culture in its very thread.

Today only one silk company remains. Garin, established in 1820, makes genuine handwoven espolín and has remained a family business since its inception. Nowadays Elena Ribes is tasked with protecting its unique heritage and craft from extinction.

"During Spain's economic downturn of 2009–2010 we were facing bankruptcy," she says. "We really didn't know how we were going to survive." A welcome solution came from the local government. Ribes sold her company's centuries-old workshop and everything in it for development into a "living" textile museum. This transformation is still in process, but the idea is that one day visitors will be able to view hundreds of hand-painted espolín pattern plans, historic documentation from Garin's former clients such as the Vatican and royal dynasties, and watch the weavers at work.

The word "espolín" refers to the podlike shuttles that cradle the threads woven over the floral designs, creating a textured effect like gold or silver brocade. Most designs require eight hours of weaving to create twenty centimeters of fabric, which later sell for one thousand euros a meter. These days, Valencia's Las Fallas festival generates most of Garin's orders, as young Valencian women compete for the title of *Fallera Mayor* wearing a traditional period costume crafted in espolín.

The Garin workshop has eleven looms and employs weavers based on demand. Although the company gets the odd request from outside Spain, most orders come from locals who understand it takes time, and money, to produce a museum-worthy length of silk.

Chapter Four

MADRID & VICINITY

MADRID & VICINITY

L ike many emblematic streets and squares, Madrid's Puerta del Sol (Gate of the Sun) is more exciting for what it represents than for what it is. Officially it's a plaza, though that's often hard to tell for the sheer quantity of foot traffic that stamps out any notion of spaciousness. But while you are here (and on any trip to Madrid you will be), make your way over to the landmark Royal House of the Post Office, look down, and you'll see a plaque on the pavement indicating you are standing at Spain's Kilometre Zero—the start and end point of six historical trade and transport routes that spanned the peninsula. Situated in the geographical center of the country, Madrid is home to Spanish royalty, the seat of government, and the most important cultural institutions. Spaniards will tell you that the most refined, sought-after, and premium of everything the country has to offer, from fine art to fresh seafood, end up here. Craft in Madrid, too, reflects a connoisseur taste, but is continually evolving for a city that has art in its DNA.

Start your handmade journey of Madrid with a stroll around the upscale Salamanca area to find bespoke tailors offering fine wool suits for the city's political class, and flagship stores of highly original Spanish housewares brands such as Sargadelos (p. 146) and Ábbatte (p. 104). Here, too, is Tado (C/ Echegaray, 31, 28014), an exquisite little boutique specializing in art pottery.

In contrast, the central historical neighborhoods of Madrid exude an old-fashioned, down-to earth authenticity unusual for a capital city. In the little flagstone streets around the magnificent Plaza Mayor, you'll find shops selling artisan basketry and rope-soled footwear, the most famous being Casa Hernanz (Calle Toledo, 18, 28005). In the hip barrio of Santa Ana, L'Officiel (C/ Santa Ana, 6, 28005) is a cornucopia of colorful ceramics from all over Iberia, including fine dinnerware from La Cartuja de Sevilla (p. 171). In La Latina every Saturday the hawkers of the El Rastro open-air flea market populate its streets with estate-sale china, terracotta cookware, and old flamenco cassettes. Here, too, is Cocol (Calle Costanilla San Andrés, 18, 28005), a truly unique shop with a beautifully curated selection of rare crafted objects from far-flung corners of Spain.

CAPAS SESEÑA

Calle de la Cruz, 23, Madrid, 28012
sesena.com · tel. + 34 915 316 840

———

Handmade capes

When chilly winds whip through Madrid, grab a cape. *Madrileños* of a certain class have been doing so for centuries. A billowy woolen cape is a symbol of *castizo* culture, the Iberian equivalent of dandyism that signifies authenticity with a sharp sartorial attitude.

In the heart of the city's *casco antiguo* (old town), Capas Seseña is reputedly the oldest specialist cape workshop in the world. Since 1901 when Santos Seseña started the business, it has made to order traditional woolen capes for Picasso, Hemingway, Fellini, countless clergy, members of royalty, and anyone with a taste for drama.

The classic Spanish cape, as seen in the company's 1901 model, has uniquely elegant characteristics. Generally made of merino wool from the region of Bejár, it is lined with contrasting cotton or velvet, features a pelerine (small cape) for extra warmth, and a silver clasp known as a "charro."

Marcos Seseña, who runs the business today, is the great grandson of Santos. Although he used to hang around the workshop when he was young, he never thought he would one day run it. But in 2009, when Spain was experiencing a deep financial downturn, Marcos decided to leave his job as a business administrator and save his family's enterprise from collapse. Since he came onboard, Capas Seseña has expanded its catalog to include ponchos and capelets with chic and contemporary stylings and lighter, even patterned fabrics. One thing that has remained constant is the means of production: each cape is still handmade by a handful of tailors at the back of the shop.

"Having our own workshop means we are constantly in production," says Santos. "We have the freedom to experiment with forms and lengths.

Making the perfect cape is actually quite complicated—it all comes down to the pattern."

For traditional capes, Santos sources wool from a company in Salamanca. "It's a special type of fabric that has a very tight weave," he explains. "The local water it is treated with has mineral properties that make it so. A tight weave is very important for a cape to keep the cold out."

For more contemporary capes, mixtures of merino and cashmere are used, lending the silhouette a modern edge that is wonderful to touch. And recent collaborations with local designers and special capsule collections have made the Spanish cape newly fashionable among the city's fashionistas.

"Most of our clients are not that wealthy but they have a keen sense of style and liked to be looked at," continues Marcos. "Many of them hail from the world of art, architecture, and performing arts." Interestingly, 40 percent of his orders come from the east coast of the United States. Which begs the question, what is it about a historical Spanish style icon that Americans find so appealing? Marcos replies, "I think a cape just makes you feel very special."

ÁBBATTE

Calle de Villanueva, 27, Madrid, 28001

abbatte.com · tel. + 34 916 225 530

———

Handmade textiles

Ábbatte is a company that makes superior quality, handwoven, and hand-dyed textiles. Perhaps no other textile brand in Spain is so completely connected to its place of origin.

Elena Goded is a biology professor who has always been interested in the reaction of natural plant dyes when applied to natural fibers. In the year 2000, she chanced upon the thirteenth-century ruins of the Monasterio de Santa María de la Sierra in the mountains of Guadarrama near Segovia. The original monastery was abandoned in the sixteenth century, and only a partial shell of the structure remained. But its spectacular setting was enough to lead Goded to inquire whether the site might be for sale. "We were told it was going to be converted into a boutique hotel," she says. "Then a year later I got a call telling me that the project had fallen through, and the site was up for sale again. I said to my family, 'This place has to have a use.'"

Around the same time Goded's daughter Camila Lanzas returned to Spain after studying fashion design in London. Mother and daughter partnered to create Ábbatte, with Goded in charge of the organic dyeing processes and Lanzas the design. Five weavers create the textiles on manual looms at the site of the old abbey, in an architect-designed workroom with views onto the sierra.

The textiles produced from Ábbatte's workshop in the mountains are mostly made for the home—linen curtains with an ethereal, gauzy quality, throws and blankets that combine merino and linen yarns, and cushion covers with subtle contrasting stripes. Elena set up a botanical garden and dye house on the property where she continues to research and experiment, resulting in hues from moss green to soft raspberry. The earthy

tones come from the unadulterated colors of baby alpaca wool, Ábbatte's signature yarn. "Absolutely everything that leaves here is completely made on-site and using manual processes," affirms Goded. "When people touch our textiles, I believe they can appreciate that."

A visit to the Ábbatte shop and showroom in the upscale Madrid neighborhood of Salamanca affirms her claim. The company's rural atelier can also be visited by appointment, and hosts courses on traditional textile crafts, from basketry to silk printing and fabric dyeing.

TOGASHI DAMASQUINOS

Toledo

damasquinados.com · tel. + 34 695 318 480

———————

Damascene jewelry and objects

Every region of Spain has a local style in the established crafts. But only one excels in a craft that's not found anywhere else. Damascene is the art of inlaying gold or silver into black steel jewelry, plates, vases, and other objects. It's an ancient decorative technique that originated in Japan and found its way to Spain with the Moors who invaded Spain in the eighth century.

The people of Toledo, which by the tenth century was no longer the capital of Spain and a melting pot of Christian, Jewish, and Arabic cultures, excelled at all metalwork. Damascene was sought after for decorating weaponry, and knowledge of the craft has since passed from generation to generation.

Today, strolling through Toledo's ancient streets, it's hard to walk five feet without being confronted with a shop window overflowing with Damascene ware. While the patterns and designs, from ancient Arabic and Christian symbols to reproductions of the old masters, look impressive, Raquel de la Torre estimates that about 60 percent of it is machine made.

De la Torre learned the art of Damascene from her (now retired) father. Today she runs a small workshop, one of the few remaining in Toledo, that produces handmade Damascene. "I used to go to my father's workplace in the afternoons and he would say, do this, try that," says the thirty-three-year-old. "So I learned little by little. I always wanted to push the craft a bit more, but he wouldn't let me."

Now the head of her own cottage business called Togashi Damasquinos, de la Torre presents a more minimalist, stylized version of Damascene than her father's. "My aim is to highlight the black background of the pieces and lend a younger, more minimalist feel," she explains. "Most Spanish Damascene is still very traditional, very *Man of La Mancha!*"

De la Torre's *taller* is set up at home, and while her finished pieces present a contemporary twist, Damascene methods have changed little. Due to the toxicity of the chemicals, the carbon steel bases are blackened at an exterior workshop. She then uses tiny chisels to embed the silver or gold wires into them. They then go back to the workshop to be briefly submerged in a mixture of caustic soda and nitrogen, which secures the metal inlay in place and leaves a polished finish. Though it can often be difficult to distinguish, handmade Damascene stands out for the brilliance of its black background, and the minute chisel markings on the inlaid metals.

De la Torre's designs come from many inspirations. Arabic symbols such as the five-pointed star continue to be in demand, and many patterns come from her own imagination. "We Damascene artisans don't have a textbook, but we have a lot of references we can refer to," she explains. "Luckily geometry is infinite."

HELENA ROHNER

Calle del Almendro, 4, Madrid, 28005
helenarohner.com · tel. + 34 913 657 906

———————

Handmade jewelry

In person, Helena Rohner is as effortlessly chic as the jewelry and objects she creates. Petite, with a short gamine haircut and dressed in fashionably minimalist attire, she greets me in her serene shop-atelier in Madrid's Latin quarter. Around her, four artisans are studiously putting together the rings, bracelets, pendants, and earrings that she exports all over the world. Rohner jumps between them while taking calls and checking the tonality of samples of bobbly ceramic beads that have just been brought in by a supplier.

Rohner is the daughter of a Swiss father and Spanish mother. She grew up in the Canary Islands, surrounded by wooden puppets made by her father and textiles woven by her mother. Despite this delightful-sounding creative environment, she decided to study politics in Florence, Italy. It was here she became interested in craft and took a jewelry course. "I discovered I wasn't so bad at it," she says. "What interested me the most was the transformation of hard materials."

She then moved to London, where she started collaborating with Jacqueline Rabun, a celebrity jeweler whose strong, contemporary pieces were forging new directions in the field. "It was through Jacqueline I realized that jewelry didn't have to be made of 'precious' materials, nor did it have to be cheap and machine-made. There is a space in-between, where other materials could be used."

Perhaps because of her mixed parentage, Rohner combines a sleek Scandinavian sensibility with a Southern European exuberance for color. From a base of gold, silver, or brass plate, she sets vividly colored ceramic stones to form precisely balanced pieces that are timeless and organic, dressing the body with curvaceous lines and delicious pops of color. "I am very much into arriving at the essence of things," she says, when asked about her ideation process. "And starting from a base of simplicity. But as I get older, I mainly just rely on my gut feelings."

While jewelry remains her mainstay medium, Rohner has expressed her now well-established artistic language in textiles, carpets, furniture, and silverware for the master Danish silversmith Georg Jensen. Her pottery line is the product of a team-building workshop they took together. "I try to keep the company alive with new challenges," she says. "I like to think we are maverick."

GUITARRAS RAMÍREZ

Calle de la Paz, 8, Madrid, 28012

guitarrasramirez.com · tel. + 34 680 122 262

Handmade guitars

"We were born in the nineteenth century, and we still have a nineteenth-century structure." Cristina Ramírez says these words with pride. She belongs to the fifth generation of the Ramírez line of guitar makers. Her great-great-great-grandfather José Ramírez founded the business in 1882. Today, her aunt Amalia is one of the first female master luthiers in Spain.

Classical and flamenco guitar-making workshops (or *Escuelas de Guitarreros*) in Spain are still structured like the ancient guilds. An apprentice has to pass through three levels before he or she becomes a *maestro*, a process that can take up to twenty years. Once they do, they are expected to break away and start their own school, continuing to impart their knowledge to new generations of guitar makers.

An atmospheric shop in Madrid's old town is the public face of the Ramiréz guitar-making dynasty. On the wall behind the wooden counter, a relic from the store's previous life as a pharmacy (the family took over the premises in 1995), handcrafted guitars with exquisite geometric inlay and lacquered finishes as brilliant as a grand piano are on display. On another wall, historic images, autographed photos of famous guitarists, and certificates of excellence affirm the Ramírez family's prominence in the highly specialized world of guitar-making.

Although a novice could come in and pick up a beginner's guitar for under five hundred euros, professional musicians have their new guitars made to order, choosing the wood, exact proportions, and the type of finish. "What a flamenco guitarist is looking for is firstly a very comfortable instrument, but also one that 'breaks' the sound a little bit, is a little rumbly," explains Cristina Ramírez. "Cypress is a wood that does that. For

classical guitars we mainly use red cedar. My grandfather was the first
to use this type of wood in the 1960s, and it then became popular all over
the world."

Once a guitar has been ordered, it will take around three months to
make in the Ramírez workshop. I ask Cristina what qualities someone
needs when learning the craft. "Very observant, patient, and with a delicate
hand," is her reply. "You need to take your time, and then it becomes, how
do you say, a spiritual experience. We have a philosophy that when you
treat an instrument like a guitar with love, it will absorb the energy."

SASTRERÍA ROQUETA

Calle Viola Manuel, 2, Utebo, Zaragoza, 50180

sastreriatoreros.com · tel. + 34 976 787 050

Bullfighting costumes

When the entertainer Madonna wanted a bullfighting suit for her 2015 tour, she contacted Sastrería Roqueta, one of the few tailors still in existence who creates the famous *traje de luces* (suit of lights) worn by Spain's matadors. With the popularity of the bullfight waning in Spain, orders from the entertainment world may be what keeps this small company afloat. "Today we received two inquiries from opera companies in the United States!" exclaims Alfredo Roqueta, who runs the business. His father Daniel (now retired) started the workshop on the outskirts of the city of Zaragoza in 1984.

Daniel Roqueta always wanted to be a matador. But he became an odd job worker traveling the country in search of opportunities. He spent a stint performing on horseback in a carnival but never made it to the bullring. Instead, he learned how to tailor from his sister-in-law, first regalia for the armed forces, before entering into the tightknit world of the *corrida* thanks to some important contacts.

The dazzlingly elegant and ornate garb of the bullfighter dates back to sixteenth-century Spain and except for a few nips and tucks hasn't evolved much. It consists of a *taleguilla*, or tight, below-the-knee trousers, and a *chaquetilla*, or heavily adorned bolero jacket. Opaque tights, a crisp white shirt, a black *montero* hat, and of course a red cape complete the dashing look.

Matadors choose the base color of his (or her) costume, often picking one they consider lucky. The decorative designs come from a catalog of century-old traditional drawings, though clients can also bring their own. Most of the embellishment—the heavy embroidery, sprays of sequins, piping, and Austrian knots—goes into the chaquetilla, an uncomfortable, rigid piece of clothing composed of seven inner layers. "Despite what many people think, the traje de luces was never designed for protection," says Alfredo. "It's totally aesthetic. The rigidity of the chaquetilla is to keep its form, the precise drape, and the perfect silhouette as the matador moves about in the ring. But if you have a run-in with a bull, it's very quickly going to get destroyed."

Although Sastrería Roqueta has incorporated some automated embroidery machines over the years, Alfredo confirms that much handwork is still required. A traje de luces takes around three months to make, and the starting price of a chaquetilla is 850 euros.

CERÁMICA SAN GINÉS TALAVERA

Calle Matadero, 7, Talavera de la Reina, Toledo, 45600
ceramicasangines.com · tel. + 34 925 818 902

————

Hand-painted tiles and tableware

Fanciful ceramic street signs and storefronts are an enchanting feature of Madrid. From wildly elaborate murals advertising tapas and medicinal formulas to nomenclature depicting historic scenes, *azulejos* (hand-painted ceramic tiles) add color and romance to Spain's towns and villages, particularly in the central and southern regions.

South of Madrid, the town of Talavera de la Reina is renowned for its local azulejos and pottery industry. The romantic yellow-and-blue "talavera style," which encompasses decorative motifs from the Roman, Moorish, and Renaissance periods, is everywhere, from monumental street fountains to numerous small workshops creating jugs, vases, plates, and plaques.

The town's prominence in ceramics is accredited to Juan Ruiz de la Luna, a polymath entrepreneur who revived the industry in the early 1900s after centuries of decline. Today, the local ceramics museum in Talavera de la Reina is named after him. Here, Mónica García del Pino, his great granddaughter, is the founder of Cerámica San Ginés Talavera, a workshop that pushes the boundaries of the medium.

"Most of the azulejos street signs you see in Madrid were created in the original workshop of Juan Ruiz de la Luna," says Pedro Bastidas, del Pino's business partner. "He also created the ceramic murals in the metro of Buenos Aires and the street signs in the French Quarter of New Orleans. There are many more gems that we are still discovering."

Cerámica San Ginés Talavera draws on this legacy by specializing in large-format architectural and urban elements in azulejos. In 2010, the company constructed a giant mural for the west facade of the Oran Convention Centre in Algiers, which the company claims is the largest hand-painted tile mural in existence. More recently, it was contacted by the renowned contemporary designer Philippe Starck to create a whimsical mural that mixes Latin and Spanish mysticism for a restaurant in Miami.

Despite receiving such highbrow commissions, Bastida claims that the local ceramics industry in Talavera de la Reina is driven not by money but by tradition, and the challenge of keeping the craft local and relevant. In the face of competition from mass-produced copies, Cerámica San Ginés Talavera refused to cut down on quality and production costs in order to stay competitive, a decision that makes their hand-painted tiles and tableware a cut above the rest.

"We have always understood that azulejos is unique," continues Bastida. "Wherever you put it, it becomes the absolute focal point. And we are also aware that the material has to last forever. In Talavera the streets are full of azulejos dating from the nineteenth century and it is perfect. The tiles haven't lost any of their color. On the contrary, over time they take on a patina and become even more attractive."

Chapter Five

BASQUE COUNTRY, LA RIOJA & CANTABRIA

BASQUE COUNTRY, LA RIOJA & CANTABRIA

Am I still in Spain? You wouldn't be the first to ask yourself this when visiting the mosaic of regions cradling the Cantabrian Sea. Secluded from the rest of the Spanish peninsula by mountain ranges, deep green valleys, and impenetrable forests, Northern Spain's unique culture is rooted in ancient fiefdoms, untainted customs, and in the case of the Basque country, its own language—Euskara.

Touring the towns and villages of the Northern Spanish regions—La Rioja, Navarra, Asturias, Cantabria, and the Basque Country—you can't help but notice how *crafted* their appearance is. From their distinct houses with their pitched roofs and overhanging balconies to the hand-cut signage written in a robust Basque font and wooden fishing boats bobbing in blustery bays, these regions have proudly clung to their cultural symbols.

Yet almost paradoxically there is a bold modernity to be found here. The shimmering Guggenheim Museum Bilbao by Frank Gehry is as arresting as it was when it first emerged in the industrial cityscape in 1997. In contrast, the city's *casco antiguo* (old town) is still bathed in gritty authenticity.

Soledad Santisteban (p. 139) and Sagarminaga (p. 133) both have their workshops here. You'll also find a smattering of pottery stores trading in rustic terracotta kitchenware and cookware.

Basque cuisine is a reference point for global gourmands, who make the elegant city of San Sebastian, with its array of renowned restaurants, a must-visit. Modern design shops displaying sleek, locally produced goodies are interspersed with heritage establishments in San Sebastian's central Ensanche district. Try on a ubiquitous Basque beret in any hat shop. Boinas Elósegui, based in Tolosa, has been making them since 1858. Although still favored by elderly Basque gentlemen, the company reached its peak in the years before the Spanish Civil War, when their berets were incorporated into the informal uniform of the freedom fighters.

In San Sebastian's *casco antiguo*, particularly near the market square, you'll find shops trading in traditional textiles, basketry, and wood, three crafts that represent the timelessness and resilience of the Northern Spanish lands.

MANTAS EZCARAY

Cristobal de Zamudio, 12, Ezcaray, 26280, La Rioja

mantasezcaray.com · tel. + 34 941 354 034

———

Woolen textiles

La Rioja is renowned throughout the world for producing fine wines, but not every part of this tiny region is covered in vineyards. Ezcaray is a handsome, well-preserved town situated in the Oja Valley and in close proximity to popular ski resorts. The valley is better known for producing woolen textiles, partly because living in mountain temperatures demands them, but also because both sheep and clear, pristine water are found here in abundance.

Mantas Ezcaray is the legacy of Cecilio Valgañon, who in 1930 set up a workshop to produce handwoven scarves, shawls, and blankets. In 1950, the company started working with mohair, the fluffy fiber made popular by pinup girls of the period.

Walking into the shop attached to the Mantas Ezcaray factory is like entering a woolly candy store. Scarves and blankets are stacked to the rafters in magenta, fuchsia, cobalt, and rust, as vibrant and alive as their original pigment. The quality and craftsmanship are what you would expect to see in a luxury department store and maybe you have, as the majority of Mantas Ezcaray's orders are for prestigious fashion houses.

"We are always looking for ways to make the colors pop out more," says Ignacio Valgañon, a descendent of the original owner. "But the strong colors are also thanks to the mohair itself, the dye really penetrates it. You can see the difference when you try the same dyes on natural wool, you don't get the same sheen."

Mohair comes from the Angora goat, and is only produced in southern Texas, southern Uruguay, Turkey, and South Africa, where Mantas Ezcaray sources. The fiber arrives at the factory raw and is then cleaned and dyed before being spun into mohair yarn.

Weaving mohair is a slow process because of the delicacy of the fiber. Tension must be kept low, and Mantas Ezcaray has set up production so there is only one weaver for every loom instead of the traditional four-to-one ratio. At full capacity the factory can produce seventy blankets a day. But the biggest obstacle is finding new weavers. "The main problem is where we are. Nobody wants to come and work in a village!" explains Valgañon, adding that most of his weavers are hitting retirement age. Digitalization of the company is also being held back through lack of time and manpower. So, for the moment, to acquire one of the exquisite textile products made by Mantas Ezcaray, you should visit their store in the village in the valley where it all started.

DAVID SANTIAGO

Bo. San Andrés, 35 – nave, San Andrés de los Carabeos, Valdeprado del Rio, 39419, Cantabria

davidsantiago.es · tel. + 34 658 339 301

———————

Woodwork

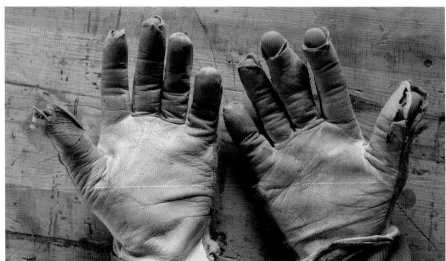

When in a restaurant in Northern Spain, please don't ask for paella. Cuisine in these parts is far away from the more popularized seafood-and-rice-based dishes you find in the Mediterranean regions. Here you will find cuisine rooted in the bounty of local farmers and fisherman prepared into hearty dishes with a holy respect for heritage and tradition—eating well in Northern Spain is next to godliness.

David Santiago is a wood craftsman in the mountainous region of Cantabria who has integrated his love of food into his work. He studied fine arts then drifted into furniture and interiors, but in 2018 worked as a baker in a well-known restaurant. He had always been interested in bread-making and the machinations of a restaurant kitchen in particular, and the experience helped define his craft. "In the sense that the skill and the doing are very much connected," he explains. "You are always trying to go a little bit further—to break molds." The first pieces to emerge from his workshop were breadboards and trowels for the bread oven. Today Santiago makes to order wooden cutlery, bowls, serving plates, salt-and-pepper mills, and other elements of the "table landscape" for Spain's best restaurants. Although exquisitely crafted and flawlessly finished, his pieces seem to express the lack of artifice that is a feature of Northern Spain's gourmet circles. They possess Japanese precision, Nordic minimalism, and natural beauty, making them perfect for the nuanced world of haute cuisine.

Santiago works alone in an isolated *nave* (industrial workshop) and mostly creates to order. At the moment, he is experimenting with cutlery crafted from *espina*, a local, wild thorn bush. He tends to work with wood that is easily and sustainably sourced, mostly oak, chestnut, and beech. Whatever the species, Santiago finishes his pieces using natural oils or beeswax and nothing more. "I was never really interested in 'artistic' crafts, the ones you see in museums and galleries," explains Santiago." I was interested more in functional handcraft, the stuff you see every day, that is within everyone's reach."

SAGARMINAGA ATELIER

Moraza Plaza, 6, bajo 3D, Bilbao, 48007
sagarminaga.com · tel. + 34 630 281 483

Natural fibers

One of the joys of driving through Spain in the late summer is seeing large cylindrical bales of hay dotting the countryside after harvest season, creating a surreal sculptural effect on the landscape. I am reminded of this when talking to Gabriela de Sagarminaga, as she is interested in the sculptural possibilities of natural vegetable fibers. She works mostly with esparto, a resilient wild grass found in abundance in arid regions of southern Spain and Morocco. From her atelier in Bilbao, she and her small team create objects and installations that give nobility to this humble material, which has historically been used for making fire torches.

After returning from Madrid, where she finished creating an installation for a new hotel situated in the neighborhood of Atocha, Sagarminaga explains, "They wanted to express something related to their location. As 'atocha' is a type of esparto, it was a good fit."

Sagarminaga, whose surname means "where the wild apples grow," studied textile technology and practiced various related disciplines before arriving at her current one. "I discovered a meeting point," she says. "It's very important to me that my work is both intellectual and manual. The intellectual part is to do with social and sustainable development. The manual part is working with my hands, which gives me a direct connection to the materials and processes."

Sagarminaga Atelier's objects approach folkloric symbols through a contemporary prism, such as *escudos* (emblems) of Basque villages and *frontales*—the decorative face protectors mounted on Andalusian horses to keep flies away. For these pieces, Sagarminaga relies on the assistance of a local weaver experienced in traditional plaiting and braiding techniques, while she focuses on researching and experimenting for larger-scale projects. "Experimenting with a 'poor man's' material gives you a lot more liberty to make errors and go in different directions," she says. "Crafted objects take a lot of time to produce. Add this to the cost of expensive materials and we see why craft has become exclusive and luxurious. I was interested in balancing this out."

But can the humility of esparto match her sophisticated creative criteria? "Yes," she answers without hesitation. "It's about reflecting on the raw material, which is natural and simple, and how with creativity and good taste you can make aesthetic pieces that elevate it."

ALBERDI MAKILA

C/ Descarga Kalea, 6, Irun, 20303

alberdimakila.com · tel. + 34 943 631 086

————

Ceremonial walking canes

Euskadi, or the Basque Country, is unique in Spain for many reasons: its impenetrable language, thought by linguists to be the oldest language isolate (unrelated to any other language) in Europe, its verdant, thickly forested landscape, and its customs and traditions.

The *makila* is a symbol of Basque culture. In essence it's a walking stick or baton but can double as a defense weapon. In Basque lore it symbolizes nobility, justice, strength, and authority, all characteristics of a people who have historically struggled to preserve their culture and "difference" against Spanish authoritarianism.

From his family home in Irun, Euskadi, Beñat Alberdi heads the only workshop that crafts traditional makilas in Spain. He has recently taken over from his father, Iñaki, now retired, who is credited with reviving the makila after it was all but erased from local memory. "In 1980 nobody knew what a makila was, it was a forgotten cultural symbol, largely because of the dictatorship," Alberdi explains, referring to the animosity Franco displayed toward the Basques during his ironfisted rule. "So in 1980 my father and uncle went to the French Basque Country, where it was still popular to learn the technique of making them. I myself learned by hanging around the workshop as a kid and working the leather, the metal, and most of all the wood for pocket money."

The makila is an intricate object that has numerous elements, all completely done by hand using manual tools and techniques that have remained unchanged for centuries.

The process starts with the selection of wood. Every spring, Alberdi sets out into local forests in search of white medlar trees. He looks for branches that are not too curved, and cuts markings (or "tattoos" as

Alberdi calls them) of curly Basque symbols into the bark. In the winter, after the tattoos have had time to "scar," he returns to cut down the branches and then store them in his workshop to dry, a process that takes ten years. When he receives an order, he retrieves a branch and straightens it on coals. He will then craft the plaited leather sheath and metal tip and handle, adding an engraving, a line of poetry or dedication in the ancient, distinctive Basque font.

Makilas are gifted on ceremonious occasions such as anniversaries, retirements, and significant birthdays. "Gifting a makila is a sign of respect," explains Alberdi. "Unlike in the rest of Spain, us Basques are not so touchy-feely. So it's a way of saying, 'I love you.'"

SOLEDAD SANTISTEBAN

C/ Costa, 8–10, 6º derecha, Bilbao, 48010

telarartesaniatextil.com · soledadsantisteban.com · tel. + 34 652 770 201

———————

Textile restoration and art

Soledad Santisteban is a veritable *maestra* of the loom. At seventy-five years old, she has long been in demand for made-to-order weaving, fine carpet restoration, macramé, and costume restoration. And that's when her nimble fingers are not creating organic sculptures from her preferred material—felt.

Santisteban's fascination for textiles began in the mid 1980s. Following a whim, she went to the southern Spanish town of Granada to buy a loom. She ended up staying for six months mastering the technique for coarsely woven, striped, and fringed curtains and throws that were popular at that time. "The hippie look was big back then, so my work found a market," she explains. "From there I learned tapestry. Then one day a man came into my studio with an antique carpet thrown over his shoulder and said, 'You make carpets don't you? So please fix this one.' That is how I entered into textile restoration, which back then was a very closed, very specialist world."

Santisteban imparts her lifelong knowledge to students in her atelier in Bilbao. When not teaching or restoring period costumes and carpets for Spanish museums, she develops her felt sculptures, which she describes as a product of her imagination and experimentation with the material.

Certainly, their abstract, organic forms are a far cry from the formality of the historic pieces she is asked to restore. Using the coarse wool from the local Latxa sheep, she washes the fibers then tints them using organic dyes. With the wool in a sodden state, she pulls, tugs, and twists the material directly on the mold, a process that requires physical strength and mental alertness. "At a given moment, a dialogue is established between the material and me," she explains. "Though sometimes it's the fabric itself that dictates the shape."

Chapter Six

GALICIA

GALICIA

Situated in the far northwestern corner of the country, Galicia is included by few tourists to Spain in their itineraries. Those that do tend to be plodding along the Camino de Santiago (the Way of Saint James), the ancient pilgrim route that ends at Santiago de Compostela—a magnificent city where the remains of Saint James are supposedly buried in its cathedral. Some may continue on to Finisterre, a remote peninsula perched on the Atlantic Ocean that is Spain's westernmost point. And perhaps others may spend a bit of time in A Coruña, Galicia's handsome capital.

But that's not to judge. Galicia has a famously rainy and overcast climate that can play havoc with holidaymaking. First inhabited by the Celts, the region also has a very different feel compared to the Latin vitality of the rest of Spain. Whipped by the Atlantic and isolated for many centuries, Galicia can feel shrouded and mysterious. Nomenclature and much conversation is in the Gallego language, and life in the mountain and rural villages appears to belong to another century.

Away from the trappings of internationalization, craft in Galicia is very local in nature. In the old streets of Santiago de Compostela, you will find an abundance of objects and filigree jewelry handmade by local silversmiths and inspired by the iconography of the Camino de Santiago, notably the ancient cross that marks the route. The emblematic enclave of Camariñas on the Costa da Morte (Coast of Death) is renowned for bobbin lacework produced by local women known as *palilleiras*. Famous for its seafood specialties, Galicia's craft and food are closely connected— from fresh Albariño wines poured into white china cups to steaming mounds of octopus served on wooden platters and ubiquitous blue-and-white tableware seen almost everywhere. For something a little different, pop into one of the numerous outlets of Bonilla a la Vista in A Coruña. The potato chips they make are a local institution and the packaging they come in exudes a maritime-modernist aesthetic that is very Galician.

A younger generation of makers, such as Idoia Cuesta (p. 150), brings a new wave to Galicia's craft scene. Others such as Sargadelos (p. 146) are so unique that they remain perpetually contemporary and begging to be discovered.

EFERRO

Rúa Riego de Agua, 4, A Coruña, 15001

elenaferro.com · tel. + 34 981 113 283

Handmade clogs

In Galicia there is a saying: *No quiero más zuecos ni pan de maiz* (I don't want any more clogs or cornbread). It's not because locals have a loathing for clogs (or indeed cornbread) particularly, but both items are associated with rural poverty and the climatic harshness of this once very isolated region of Spain.

In the case of clogs, Elena Ferro is successfully working toward turning this mindset around. Clogs have always been part of her life. Her family's artisan clog workshop has been making zuecos for three generations and is still standing thanks to Ferro's creative flair and vision.

Though not generally thought of as Spanish, clogs were traditionally worn by farmers for protection against snow and Galicia's famously damp weather. By the 1970s, as Spain was entering the modern world, they fell out of favor and were replaced by rubber boots. Ferro learned the clog-making trade from the ground up—working in her family's workshop after school and eventually taking over the business. Realizing that she had to innovate to survive, she began experimenting with designs, finishes, and colors. Thanks to social media she steadily built a following. Eferro, her brand, is still produced in her family's original workshop near the ancient township of Pontevedra. She also has a standalone store in A Coruña.

With their funky shapes, vivid colors, and chunky laces, Ferro's clogs may look worlds apart from their predecessors, but their composition and structure has changed little. "The main point of difference is the type of wood," she explains. "We now use lighter woods for a more urban context. We are also developing an articulated sole that will aid with flexibility."

Part of Ferro's mission is to keep the skill of Galician clog-making alive. "There are only five workshops left," she notes. "Anything handmade has to tell the story behind it. And that's what we are trying to do."

SARGADELOS

Rúa Real, 56, A Coruña, 15003
sargadelos.com · tel. + 34 981 222 604

————

Porcelain objects and tableware

When enjoying octopus, clams, and oysters at one of Galicia's famed seafood restaurants, or simply having a drink in a local bar, it doesn't take long to notice that cups, plates, and even beer taps are decorated with distinctive cobalt-and-white geometric patterns. The style, which references Celtic symbolism and folklore, is as ubiquitous to Galicia as sea fog.

The inventor of these intriguing objects is Sargadelos, a company that was founded in 1804 in the village of the same name. Its porcelain tableware is intrinsically entwined in Galician history and cultural renaissance.

In the 1960s, a group of Galician intellectuals returned to their homeland after migrating to Argentina to escape General Franco's rule. They set up an institute called the Laboratorio de Formas (Laboratory of Forms). Its aim was to regain Galicia's "historic memory"—the knowledge of local culture, in all its forms, that General Franco had tried so hard to wipe from the collective consciousness. It did this through publications in the Gallego language, art seminars, workshops, and the revival of the Sargadelos pottery plant as a beacon of Galician identity.

Today, Sargadelos has two production plants employing over two hundred craftspeople carrying out largely the same processes that were used over a century ago. Firstly, liquid kaolinite—the principal material in porcelain production that creates sheen and translucence—is poured into the mold and then pre-cooked. The form is then detailed, refined, and decorated before being glazed in a high-temperature "tunnel" oven for eight hours. From start to finish the process can take as much as a day per piece, with each step executed by a craftsperson specialized in the task at hand.

The majority of the Sargadelos designs hail from the time of the artists involved in the Laboratorio de Formas. From this period, a version of a

"Toby jug" is painted with abstract faces of Galician historical figures. Other figurines depict Galician carnival and folkloric characters, political commentators and intelligentsia, indigenous flora, and vernacular architectural forms.

While in more recent years the company has branched out into lifestyle products such as textiles and candles, its mainstay is, and probably always will be, its dazzling cobalt-and-white tableware. Galicia is known as a region of immigrants, and a piece of Sargadelos is often gifted to the departing as a reminder of their homeland. Before leaving Galicia, it would be foolish not to partake in this ritual for yourself.

IDOIA CUESTA

Outeiro de Rei, Lugo, 27150

idoiacuesta.com · tel. + 34 677 334 150

Natural fiber art and objects

Today, Idoia Cuesta is a little frazzled. She has just returned from Valencia, where she gives classes as part of a master's course in design. Shortly, she will be off again to the Salone del Mobile, Milan's renowned furniture and design fair where some of her pieces will be exhibited. "Lately I have been traveling a lot!" she says. "But I am lucky enough to have this place to come back to, this haven of peace."

Cuesta creates baskets, sculptures, installations, and objects by weaving, knotting, and interlacing natural fibers. The haven of peace she refers to is her home and workshop in the depths of a biosphere reserve in rural Galicia, a place that is her constant source of inspiration.

Cuesta entered the world of basketry in a roundabout way. She wanted to be a biologist, but always dabbled in various artisan crafts on the side. Basketry got her hooked. She moved to Galicia, where basketry is a craft that is quite visible in everyday life, to finish her biology course. She ended up spending as much time studying and investigating traditional weaving methods as living organisms. At thirty years old, after she finished her biology course, she decided to change direction. Twenty years later, she is one of the few artisans in Spain who has successfully managed to cross over into the realm of design and art. Her collections, which have grown beyond baskets to large-scale objects and sculptures, are in demand, not only by private clients but also luxury brands that commission her for in-store installations and special projects. I ask her about the moment she made the jump from utilitarian objects (baskets) to artistic pieces:

"Well, I do continue to make utilitarian objects," she replies. "That is to say, collections that have a specific use. Making the prototype is fun. But then what happens? You enter into the production phase and boredom sets in. So I try to look for a balance between useful objects and 'magic moments'—pieces that are more artistic."

One of these flashes of inspiration happened when she entered a traditional shop selling fisherman's gear. She found a type of nylon rope that captured her interest for its color, translucence, and plasticity—all qualities absent from the grasses and reeds she normally works with. The result of this discovery is the Abisal collection—a series of anemone-like sculptures that reference her knowledge of sea biology. Other inspiration comes from land-based natural phenomena, such as her signature *nido* (nest) method of folding, bending, and twisting her material into giant forms reminiscent of the stork nests you see all over Galicia.

"Sometimes I let the material dictate the form and other times I have to look for a material for a particular shape," she answers when asked about her creative process. "I have a million pictures in my head, but I learned early on that it's not necessary to think too much about where the piece came from, or even why."

ATALANTA MADERA

Lugar Mouteira, 10, Berres, Pontevedra, 36688

atalantamadera.es · tel. + 34 986 588 688

———————

Wooden housewares

For centuries, Berros, a municipality by the River Ulla has been known as a place of woodturners. Nobody really knows why, but what is certain is that an abundance of tree species grows along the riverbanks, from oak to chestnut to graceful silver birches. As historical land ownership records show, the surname Neira has been associated with the craft in Berros since 1808. Today, after the death of their father, sisters Ana and Isabel Neira manage the family workshop started by their great-great-grandfather.

"Masculine? Well, I guess you could say, with the exception of dress-making, all traditional crafts are masculine," answers Isabel when I comment that it's unusual to find a heritage woodworking business headed by two women. "But it caused me great sadness to think that this craft, that has been in our family for over two hundred years, would disappear with our father's passing. And anyway, I have always been quite stubborn."

Working together, Ana and Isabel create simple yet exquisitely crafted housewares under the name Atalanta. Their range focuses on utilitarian pieces for the kitchen, presentation dishes and platters, spatulas, scoops, and a nutcracker, which by a twist of fate ended up for sale in the shop of London's Tate Modern. Perhaps their most unique piece is the panera— a traditional receptacle to store flour and/or leave bread dough to rise in, normally a standalone piece in country homes. Ana and Isabel created a mini version minus the legs for use in modern kitchens and made tweaks to the lids so it could double as an attractive serving tray.

While Isabel, who has a background in art history, takes care of the design and finishing and day-to-day company business, Ana crafts the pieces with traditional manual lathes, gauges, and chisels left behind by her forefathers. "I don't normally say this, but I admire what Ana has achieved so much because our father, her *maestro*, died just as she was starting to learn the trade," says Isabel. "So really she is self-taught."

Ana pushes back modestly. "Well, it's a bit like when immigrants arrived in the Wild West and learned the lay of the land little by little. First, they got a cow, then they had a farm. I am happy with what I have achieved, but there is always something more to learn."

Chapter Seven

ANDALUSIA

ANDALUSIA

When we think of Andalusia, it's difficult not to fall into clichés. We conjure images of whitewashed villages where balconies heave with colorful bougainvillea and geraniums, dashing *señoritas* dressed in swathes of polka dots and lace, cobblestoned streets where the scent of jasmine envelopes the air, and grand Arabic landmarks such as the Alhambra that evoke a thousand and one nights. To the delight of visitors, all of this is true.

Within vast boundaries that contain stunning coastlines and majestic high countries, *pueblos blancos*, and ancient fortresses, Andalusia is archetypal Spain. Folklore and tradition are entwined into every facet of everyday life, from the endless calendar of religious celebrations to the pageantry of the equestrian arts and the intoxicating sound and vision of flamenco music. While popular destination cites such as Cádiz, Malaga, Seville, and Córdoba have naturally developed a modern edge, a unique breed of Spanish exoticism is always bubbling under the surface.

Local craft is to be found everywhere in Andalusia, but particularly in the shops and markets of the historic quarters.

Seville is especially bountiful. The streets of Santa Cruz, the compact, romantic neighborhood to the east of the city's cathedral, are packed with little specialty shops full of enticing knickknacks. To get the swirly, ruffled, flamenco-inspired look, Lina 1960 (C/ Lineros, 17, 41004) makes divine dresses and accessories from its own workshop for Spanish stars and celebrities. Francisco López Galán, owner of the leather workshop Guarnicionería López (C/ Moratín, 32, 41001), is a wanted man by Spanish royalty for his hunting goods, travel bags, and iconic riding boots. Over in Malaga, Artesanía Florencia (C/ Santa Lucía, 7, 29008) has been creating exquisite lace *mantillas* (head scarves) and bridal veils since 1952. And if you find yourself in Artarfe, near Granada, do pop into the showroom of Cerámica Los Arrayanes (Carretera de Córdoba, 430, 18230) for rustic-chic pottery emblazoned with bold floral motifs.

JOSÉ LUIS BAZÁN

Barrio Nazarí, Benaocaz, Cádiz, 11612

joseluisbazan.com · tel. + 34 643 430 750

———

Leather objects

José Luis Bazán is known as the "alchemist of leather." This reputation is born from the way he manipulates animal skins to appearances and forms not generally associated with the material: surfaces as smooth as fine porcelain, as rigid as metal, and in hues as deep as dyed silk. The visual language he has developed over his award-winning career is sophisticated, minimalist, and very much in demand in the luxury home decor and craft collectors market.

Yet there is an intriguing disconnect between the creator and his high-end creations. Dressed in a rustic checked lumberman's shirt and peaked cap, Bazán is impish, irreverent, and direct. His workshop is attached to his isolated home in the hills above Cádiz, the whitewashed capital of the Costa de la Luz (Coast of Light). He describes it as "total anarchy."

Bazán is completely self-taught. His introduction into the world of leather crafting happened in the workshops of his father. (His grandfather, who was murdered by fascist soldiers during the Spanish Civil War, was also in the trade.) By the time he turned eighteen, Bazán had started his own business with a group of friends. From the beginning, he has been researching, experimenting, and pushing the material to its limits.

Bazán mostly uses the "wet mold" process. He sculpts bowls, boxes, trays, and other objects by pinning down and then shaping the pelts over solid wooden casts. To achieve strength and rigidity, he uses up to six layers of leather before placing soft lambskin for the outer layers. With the help of an apprentice, he completes about fifteen to twenty pieces a month, though a faulty pelt means he must often start over from scratch.

"Each of my pieces has its own story to tell," he says. "Even if I make a hundred of the same object, each and every one will have a different energy. This is the real value of craft."

THE EXVOTOS

C/ Castellar, 33, Seville, 41003
theexvotos.com · tel. + 34 670 586 609

————

Ceramic objects and decor

The Exvotos is a ceramics brand formed by the partnership between Luciano Galán and Daniel Maldonado. The name refers to the offerings left in places of worship—wax limbs, sacred heart amulets, and Mexican *retablos* that are found throughout Catholic culture and folklore.

"We use them as a source of inspiration," says Galán from his workshop in Seville. "In Andalusia every fiesta is based in religion. Everything revolves around the cult of the Virgin. But the symbolism is much older. It stems from the Romans and it's very mixed with paganism and the cultures that existed in Iberia before Catholicism."

Galán and Maldonado possess a palpable southern Spanish lust for life and a lightning quick way of expression. Both studied diverse artistic techniques before founding their business in the year 2000. Maldonado went to Lisbon to learn pottery and restoration, while Galán spent time in Venice learning the art of the *mondonovo maschere*—the carnivalesque papier-mâché masks the city is famous for. Their eclectic training and interest in ancient cultures and crafts has led to a singular style—a glorious, expressive mishmash that has drawn a cultish legion of fans across the world. Currently, there is an eight-month waiting list for one of their signature heads—planters or vases that resemble female faces wearing goddess-like adornments. Specialist decor shops that stock their work can sell out of shipments in a few hours.

Despite the high demand, Galán and Maldonado reject the idea of taking on extra help. "The thing is, we work in a very intimate way. Our greatest wish is to live like monks," Galán admits. The pair work tirelessly and share all tasks between them, starting with the projection of a new piece in watercolor to a plaster mock-up to perfect dimensions. The details—

the delicate ears, ornate headpieces, necklaces, and expressive faces—are all done by hand, making each piece unique. "We approach each piece as a work of art," continues Galán. "Which is why we need to have complete control. We believe there is a lot of smoke and mirrors in the art and craft worlds these days. We aim to create something that is absolutely authentic."

"Anyway," he concludes. "We are not here to be rich. We are here to be happy."

BORDADOS JESÚS ROSADO

C/ Zamorano, 36, Écija, Seville, 41400
jesusrosado.com · tel. + 34 955 902 823

Art embroidery and restoration

Most Spanish adolescent boys opt for soccer or learning a foreign language as an after-school activity. Jesús Rosado chose embroidery. The son of a carpenter, Rosado says he has always been attracted to the world of fashion and textiles. The art of embroidery, with its high level of concentration and exacting methodology, is often described as monastic. When he was fourteen years old, Rosado entered into this highly specialized world as an apprentice in a workshop run by Philippine nuns. Today he is one of the few specialists in Spain in what is known as art embroidery.

His own workshop is situated in a spectacular Andalusian-style patio in his hometown of Écija. Here, sixteen women (whom Rosado affectionately refers to as *las niñas*) work at communal tables restoring ancient embroidered ceremonial cloths, flags, and regalia for museums and cultural foundations, or create new ones for the celebrations and street processions of the *cofradías* (Catholic fraternities) of southern Spain.

"Most of the commissions we receive fall into the 'sacred art' category," Rosado clarifies. "But we also receive requests from creators of haute couture and bullfighting costumes too. For the first time, we have just created our own line of bags. Then of course there are the brides!"

One of Rosado's more celebrated works is the creation of a backdrop for the Santa Faz de Córdoba, a task that took years of research for the correct base textile, which was eventually found in Italy. Another is the baroque, gold-threaded motifs on a velvet tunic worn by an effigy of Christ that has become the star attraction of the passionate *Semana Santa* (Easter) processions in the southern Spanish city of Huelva.

Given this elevated religious and cultural significance, I ask Rosado if the "monastic" trope applies to the ambiance of his workshop. "Not really," is his reply. "It's true that a lot of concentration is required. But the atmosphere is very communal and there is a lot of chatter and a lot of laughter. Remember that apart from myself we are all women. So we mostly talk about food."

LA CARTUJA DE SEVILLA

Ctra. Nacional, 630, km 805, Salteras, Seville, 41909

lacartujadesevilla.com · tel. + 34 955 997 952

————

Fine china tableware

In 1841 the Englishman Charles Pickman had a dream. The son of a successful trader in ceramics from Staffordshire, the traditional home of British pottery, he relocated to Seville with the idea of setting up a tableware factory with the same processes and romantic decorative style produced in his home country.

By a fortuitous twist of fate, Pickman found a stellar location. His move to Seville coincided with a royal decree that forced Spain's ancient monasteries to be vacated for private (and therefore tax-paying) use. With this, Pickman was able to secure the fourteenth-century Monasterio de Santa María de las Cuevas, located on La Cartuja, a small island on Seville's Guadalquivir River, for his new venture. He named his business La Cartuja de Sevilla.

Pickman's dream flourished. He implemented modern production methods such as molds, presses, and high-temperature ovens, and trained locals in the art of making fine china. He sought to compete with the best English pottery firms by producing high-quality tableware decorated with a Willow-pattern style of intricate pastoral scenes. And he succeeded. La Cartuja de Sevilla became an official supplier to the Spanish and other royal courts across Europe before being successfully exported to Latin America and beyond. The tableware of La Cartuja de Sevilla reached iconic status in the homes of southern Spanish gentry, and even today local historians credit Pickman with bringing the industrial revolution to southern Spain.

By the middle of the twenty-first century, however, the company was in dire straits. Along with changing tastes, the structure set up by Pickman a century ago had failed to modernize significantly. In 1971 the Monasterio de Santa María de las Cuevas was re-appropriated (it is now the Centro Andaluz de Arte Contemporáneo) and the company was forced to set up new premises on the outskirts of Seville. By 2001, debt to the Spanish state in the form of unpaid taxes was so great that the company was forced to hand over its vast historical archive to the Ministry of Culture, which then dispersed it to various museums.

"We were in love with the brand, so, yes, the reasons we bought it were probably more sentimental," says Ana Zapata, whose family acquired the business in 2011. "It has formed part of our lives. We have so many memories of being gathered around the table with La Cartuja."

Zapata and her team are steering La Cartuja de Sevilla in contemporary directions. Legacy designs are still bestsellers but added to the mix is eye-popping imagery from some of Spain's of-the-moment illustrators. "Everybody wants to work with us," claims Zapata. "Looking for collaborations and synergies is now a big part of what we do."

The company has adapted its products in other ways, too, by offering single plates, smaller sets, and more lifestyle pieces. "We have adapted the forms to modern living," continues Zapata. "Nobody has the space, or the need, for a twelve-place dinner set anymore. We are very aware of that."

While design and company infrastructure have thankfully changed, Zapata confirms that the seventy artisans she employs still use magisterial processes. The pieces stand out for the vivacity and depth of their decoration. "Fine china is a lot more durable than porcelain," says Zapata. "The colors will never, ever fade." Part of her job has been overseeing the digitalization of the company's archive of designs, some of which have never been put into production. You can see a selection of these and other historic pieces in a small display room on the factory premises, where you might also pick up some imperfect but bargain-priced pieces at the factory outlet.

Though the business is not quite out of the red yet, Zapata is optimistic that La Cartuja de Sevilla will once again see glory days. She is excited that her company has signed a new contract with the Spanish royal family to supply gifts for visiting dignitaries and has high hopes for the export market. "And anyway," she finishes, "la Cartuja has always risen up from the ashes."

JARAPAS HILACAR

C/ Carretera, 29, Bubión, 18412, Granada
jarapahilacar.com · tel. + 34 658 106 576

—————

Jarapa rugs

Although Andalusia is famed as a Mediterranean destination, there are mountains to be enjoyed too. The Alpujarra region forms part of the Sierra Nevada, the snow-topped mountains whose majestic peaks include mainland Spain's highest point. The Alpujarra is located on the range's lower slopes. Melting snow has given birth to an abundance of springs and streams, making the landscape green and fertile most of the year. Olive and almond groves and citrus fruit proliferate on irrigated terraces surrounding picturesque whitewashed villages with a distinct Arabic feel, as the Alpujarra was first populated by the Muslim Spanish people of Al-Andalus.

The village of Bubión is more colorful than most. *Jarapas*, a type of thick, rustic weave rug, hang from almost every storefront and balcony, swathing the village in vivid geometric patterns. Jarapa-making is also a legacy of the region's Moorish past, when jarapas were used as blankets to keep warm through snowy winters. Most of the jarapas on sale in Bubión today, however, are imports from either Morocco or Portugal.

Jarapas Hilacar is the sole remaining jarapa workshop in the Alpujarra. It is run by Ana Martínez, who came to Bubión in 1990 to learn the craft and then stayed. Traditionally, jarapas were a way of reusing old sheets, towels, and other household textiles by cutting them into strips. (*Jarapa* is derived from the word *harapo*, which means a torn piece of clothing or rag.) Martínez sources her raw material among cotton offcuts from textile factories. Yet the overall look and feel of her jarapas still retain a rustic, handmade charm.

Working alone, Martínez can weave about eight small jarapas a day, though she often receives orders for rugs as long as five meters. She also gives classes in basic jarapa-making whereby the textile strips are pushed by hand through a warp thread mounted on a loom. "People learn very quickly," she assures. "And the thickness of the strips means they can always walk away with a finished piece."

Martínez tries to dedicate time to innovating with new forms such as curtains and bags that have been added to her collection. But talking with her leaves the overall impression that the culture of jarapas will remain as resistant to change as the Alpujarra region itself.

Martínez, who is sixty years old, has no apparent heir to her business. She is hoping that someone will offer to buy it before she retires. "There are still a few years to go," she says. "But I am hoping someone will come along and get hooked on jarapas as I did. But the future is always uncertain. Better to focus on the present."

Acknowledgments

The creation of this book was a journey, and there were many people that supported me along the way. I would sincerely like to thank Jan Hartman for initially pushing the idea through, my editor Jennifer Thompson for her graciousness and unending patience, Jane Riley for her visual input, and every artisan I interviewed, who, true to the character of Spain, were always so generous with their time and stories.

I dedicate this book to my daughter Sadiatu, who is the most creative person I know.

Credits

Front and back cover: Courtesy Huguet
Inside front cover: Courtesy Sargadelos

6–7: Courtesy Ábbatte
8: Courtesy Cocol
10: Courtesy Sargadelos
18–21: Jara Varela
22: Courtesy Cocuan
24–27: Courtesy Estudi Ribaudí
28: Courtesy Marc Monzó
31–33: Courtesy Mietis
35: Jordi Ramis
36–39: Courtesy Norman Vilalta
40–43: Courtesy Octaevo
44: Courtesy PARDOhats
47–49: Miquel Llonch
54: Courtesy Xavier Monclús
57–59: Courtesy Studio Jaia
60: Styled by Bonvivant_concept

62–63: Courtesy Adriana Meunié
65–67: Courtesy Huguet
69: Courtesy Majoral
71–73: Courtesy Teixits Riera
74–77: Courtesy Carmina Shoemaker
83–85: Courtesy Vicente Gracia
87–89: Feminim
90: Amado Bimbo
92–95: Courtesy Garin
100–103: Guille Sola
105–107: Paco Marín
109: Courtesy Togashi Damasquinos
110: Courtesy Helena Rohner
112–115: Courtesy Guitarras Ramírez
116: Courtesy Sastrería Roqueta
118–121: Courtesy Cerámica San Ginés Talavera

127–129: Courtesy Mantas Ezcaray
130: Courtesy David Santiago
132–135: Néstor Errea
137: Courtesy Alberdi Makila
138: Courtesy Soledad Santisteban
144: Courtesy Eferro
147–149: Courtesy Sargadelos
151–154: Lorena Grandío
155: Patricia Figueiras
161: Courtesy José Luis Bazán
162–165: Sonia Fraga
167–169: Courtesy Jesús Rosado
170–173: Courtesy La Cartuja de Sevilla
175: Courtesy Jarapas Hilacar